Praise for

VANISHING POINT

"At a moment when Americans feel a deep unease about the future of their democracy, Edwin Hagenstein names the phenomenon with precision—'constitutional jitters'—and explores it with rare balance and insight. *Vanishing Point* is a refreshingly even-handed examination of how we got here and where the Constitution might take us next. Hagenstein offers readers from every background a clear-eyed map through today's constitutional anxieties."

> DIANE HESSAN, author of *Our Common Ground: Insights from Four Years of Listening to American Voters*

"Meeting our current political moment with even-handed grace, Edwin Hagenstein brings a much-needed open-mindedness to the varying, complex perspectives of the Constitution. Applying a multifaceted lens to constitutional scholarship, *Vanishing Point* is for anyone seeking both facts and hope to face our nation's current challenges."

> NEAL SIMON, author of *Contract to Unite America* and 2018 independent candidate for U.S. Senate

RealClear
Publishing

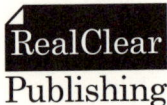

www.amplifypublishinggroup.com

Vanishing Point: In Search of Our Constitutional Future

For more information, please contact:
RealClear Publishing, an imprint of Amplify Publishing Group
620 Herndon Parkway, Suite 220
Herndon, VA 20170
info@amplifypublishing.com

Library of Congress Control Number: 2025904682
CPSIA Code: PRV0525A
ISBN-13: 979-8-89138-604-4

Printed in the United States

To my brothers and my sister: Jonathan Phillips Hagenstein, Randall Hill Hagenstein, and Elizabeth Ann Hagenstein.

Edwin C. Hagenstein

VANISHING POINT

*In Search of Our
Constitutional Future*

RealClear
Publishing

CONTENTS

PREFACE

The idea for this book crystallized early in 2021, in the wake of the January 6 assault on the Capitol. I found the spectacle of that day unnerving, especially coming as it did on the heels of the previous year, with its many distresses and disturbances: COVID, rioting after George Floyd's death, and more. For me, what came from that period was a serious case of constitutional jitters, a sense that something was wrong not just with specific policy choices we were making or with political stand-offs of the moment. All the bad news pointed to a problem closer to the foundations of our order. In the effort to see our underlying predicament more clearly, I chose to step back from the current political strife and look at those foundations, and especially at the way our constitutional choices over the course of decades led to this moment.

Hopefully, this effort to step back has led to clearer thinking on my part about our long-term constitutional health and is reflected in this book, but I hope at the same time that this stepping back has not led to a disconnect with our daily political convulsions. Interestingly, as I write during the first weeks of Donald Trump's second presidency, the newsworthy flare-ups often have a constitutional dimension: the legitimacy of the Department of Government Efficiency (DOGE), which was not created by an act of Congress; President Trump's authority to re-shape federal agencies according to the DOGE's suggestions; or, by contrast, the authority of Congress over those agencies, given that it funds them, (presumably) to accomplish its will; or, yet again, the authority of federal judges in district courts to block Trump from enforcing his plans for the bureaucracy, including the large part within the executive branch of which he is chief. All of these issues are at least indirectly addressed in the pages of this book. (Another serious quandary—the legitimacy of the previous president's pardons, apparently signed with an "auto-pen"—was entirely unforeseen!)

However important such immediate challenges might be, this book also addresses our complicated political impasse at a deeper level, exploring questions of the ultimate authority of our laws and even future of our constitutional order. Whatever the outcome of our current multifaceted strife may be, we will face underlying challenges for the foreseeable future, whether we like it or not.

INTRODUCTION

Legal scholars sometimes speak of *constitutional moments,* those times when conflicting political ideals are on a collision course and the clash can neither be avoided nor survived without dramatic change. Two examples are often cited: (1) the Civil War and its aftermath, with the Thirteenth, Fourteenth, and Fifteenth amendments; and (2) the mid-1930s and the Supreme Court's acceptance of the New Deal, with its heavy expansion of government power into the nation's economic life.

Given the state of politics in the United States today, a question naturally arises: Are we facing our own constitutional moment? There is surely something in the air, a rising of political temperatures, the sense of looming trouble just out of sight. But if we are facing a constitutional moment, it is a strange one. It differs from the two mentioned above in its murkiness, its lack of definition. In the wake of the Civil War, the stakes were widely understood—the fate of the old South and its institutions vs. the rights of freed slaves and the power of the Union. Likewise, there was plenty of clarity on what was at stake when the Supreme Court grappled with Franklin Roosevelt's domestic program: How much regulatory power can the federal government legitimately claim? At present, however, while we have plenty of political animosity and people choosing sides right and left, it is hard to identify a key, defining issue that is being fought over, one that might result in a constitutional amendment, say, or an ambitious legislative program that would steer the ship of state in some new direction. There are lots of challenges in the air, including immigration, free speech, the power of the administrative state, perhaps even the fate of democracy, as Democratic campaigners put it during the 2024 presidential election. But the high political animosity of our time has the feel of stray voltage, ready to burst into blue flame when it touches one or another issue, yet lacking any clear focal point.

Still, whatever the constitutional stakes may be, that voltage is high, and recent years have delivered enough undeniably bad tidings to give millions of Americans a strong sense that something is troubled, perhaps deeply, in our constitutional republic. There was, for instance, the unsettling (first) presidency of Donald Trump. An anomaly among presidents, he was more a businessman by background than a man of public affairs, and as much an entertainer as a businessman. He was embraced by tens of millions of voters,[1] to whom his bull-in-the-china-shop ways appealed enormously. Trump's supporters wanted Washington, and our politics generally, shaken up, and Trump delivered. In the process, he was impeached twice, setting a record unlikely to be matched anytime soon.

Toward the end of the first Trump administration, American public life took another jarring turn when the "novel" COVID-19

---

[1] And absolutely loathed by other millions.

virus began to infect large numbers of people. Many thousands reportedly died from (or at least with) COVID-19 in 2020 and the total would ultimately surpass one million.[2] The pandemic led to aggressive containment policies, enacted at the federal, state, and local levels. Often these policies were implemented through executive orders using emergency powers, rather than through legislative processes. They included demands for masking, social distancing, and lockdowns, all of which proved highly disruptive to ordinary affairs, including, crucially, life in the public schools.

The disturbances of 2020, however, were only getting started when COVID hit. In May of that year, George Floyd, an unarmed Black man, died after being brutally restrained by police in Minneapolis, Minnesota, having been pulled over in a traffic stop. Video of the event went viral online and sparked widespread protests. Sometimes riotous, the unrest spread to 140 municipalities in the United States and even some abroad. Lasting for months in cities such as Portland, Oregon, the rioting resulted in roughly twenty-five deaths in the month after Floyd's death, with a financial toll that rose to around $2 billion.[3]

There was something uncanny about these ongoing calamities that left Americans rattled and with the sense that something might

---

[2] Statista, "Total Number of Cases and Deaths from COVID-19 in the United States as of April 26, 2023," https://www.statista.com/statistics/1101932/coronavirus-covid19-cases-and-deaths-number-us-americans/.

[3] In terms of damages, the data are difficult to pin down, but see: Lois Beckett, "At Least 25 Americans Were Killed During Protests and Political Unrest in 2020," *The Guardian*, October 31, 2020, https://www.theguardian.com/world/2020/oct/31/americans-killed-protests-political-unrest-acled. Brad Polumbo, "George Floyd Riots Caused Record-Setting $2 Billion in Damage, New Report Says. Here's Why the True Cost Is Even Higher," Foundation for Economic Education, September 16, 2020, https://fee.org/articles/george-floyd-riots-caused-record-setting-2-billion-in-damage-new-report-says-here-s-why-the-true-cost-is-even-higher/.

be seriously wrong with the country. To a nation on edge, confirmation of such fears arrived on January 6, 2021, the day Congress met to formally certify the Electoral College count from the 2020 vote, thus confirming Joe Biden's election as President of the United States. On that day, protesters gathered in large numbers at the Capitol, responding to outgoing President Trump's claim that the results were cooked. A sizable number rushed the entrance and occupied the building illegally. Some gained entry to the offices of various members of Congress, others forced their way onto the floor of the House of Representatives and enjoyed posturing in the Speaker's seat, while others lounged about the Senate chamber. The intrusion was sometimes violent and in the ensuing chaos one protester was shot and killed, and more than a hundred police officers were injured.

This attack on the Capitol during such crucial and sensitive business—the peaceful transfer of power—was a shock to millions of Americans who watched in disbelief as events unfolded. Heavily armed Special Weapons And Tactics (SWAT) teams slowly cleared the building, while the mayor of Washington, DC called a curfew to take effect that evening, and the National Guard of Virginia was called out to enforce order in and around the Capitol.

On the evening of the sixth, after the mob had been dispersed, disgust with the event appeared virtually universal. When Congress reconvened to finish certifying the election, individual speakers from both parties rose to express their disdain for the mob. Elsewhere, recently resigned Secretary of Defense James Mattis, who had served under President Trump, also denounced the events and placed blame on his one-time superior: "Today's violent assault on our Capitol, an effort to subjugate American democracy by mob rule, was fomented by Mr. Trump."[4] Within hours many members of the media, including prominent conservatives, were calling for the immediate impeachment of the president (this would be his second). In an effort to calm the nation, President-elect Joe Biden released a video statement in which he, too, denounced the occupation of the Capitol, but also emphasized a particular message: "The scenes of chaos in the Capitol do not reflect the true America, do not represent who we are."[5]

Biden's claim—that's not who we are—served a useful purpose in the moment. But on reflection it raised an obvious question. If that was not who we are, who was it, and, for that matter, who are we? Though the mob was not representative of all America, it was just as surely a real slice of America on display. Despite some clear eccentrics in the mix, the protesters seemed on the whole to be ordinary citizens. The protester who died from wounds at the demonstration, Ashli Babbitt, had served in the Air Force, ran a small business with her husband, and apparently voted for Barack Obama at least once—hardly the profile of a radical.[6] Not radical by nature, but perhaps radicalized in the disorienting events of

---

[4] Luis Martinez, "Former Defense Secretary Mattis says Trump 'fomented' the security breach at the US Capitol," *ABC News*, January 6, 2021, https://abc-news.go.com/Politics/defense-secretary-mattis-trump-fomented-security-breach-us/story?id=75100611.

[5] WBUR Newsroom, "TRANSCRIPT: 'It's Not Protest, It's Insurrection': Biden Delivers Remarks on 'Siege' Upon US Capitol," *WBUR*, January 6, 2021, https://www.wbur.org/news/2021/01/06/transcript-joe-biden-capitol-chaos.

[6] Wikipedia, "Killing of Ashli Babbitt," https://en.wikipedia.org/wiki/Killing_of_Ashli_Babbitt.

recent years, and somehow indicative of something coming unte-
thered in American society.

Trust in our institutions is plummeting across the board, including government, business, and education. In a major Gallup poll,
only 27 percent of Americans report feeling either a great deal or
quite a lot of confidence in government's fundamental offices and
agencies, with the presidency registering just 23 percent and Congress a remarkable 7 percent.[7] In a democratic nation, dependent
on broad-based support for our constitutional order, this deterioration seems at least problematic and likely unsustainable.

Also indicative of deep-seated trouble is the way in which the
events of January 6 were interpreted in their aftermath. Over the
weeks that followed, millions of Americans, largely Democratic
Party members, came to the conclusion that the demonstrators that
day were not simply a mob, but participants in an insurrection. On
the one-year anniversary, President Biden spoke harshly about that
day's events, describing them as "a dagger at the throat of democracy" adding that the people of the United States were in "a battle
for the soul of America."[8]

This insistence was some distance from his claim that the mob
did not reflect the true America and amounted to upping the rhe-
torical ante. This bid was met and raised, as opponents of the
Democrats began to claim that the charge of insurrection itself was
an act of political aggression. According to this line of thought,

[7] Lydia Saad, "Historically Low Faith in Institutions Continues," Gallup, July
6, 2023, https://news.gallup.com/poll/508169/historically-low-
faith-institutions-continues.aspx.

[8] Brian Naylor, "Transcript: Biden, Harris Remarks on Anniversary of Jan. 6
Capitol Insurrection," NPR, January 6, 2022, https://www.npr.
org/2022/01/06/1069979415/biden-harris-jan-6-insurrection-speech.

equating the January 6 protest with insurrection was a ploy to smear Trump supporters across the board, to define support for him as politically unacceptable, and to justify its suppression. Conservative commentator Roger Kimball described the January 6 action as a political protest that "got out of hand," lasting just a few hours, causing relatively little property damage, and resulting in only one direct death, that of the protester shot by the Capitol Hill police.[9] Gadfly Glenn Greenwald, many of whose barbs have been aimed at conservatives over the years, worried that claims of insurrection would lead to serious incursions against civil liberties. If the United States really was under threat from right-wing insurrectionists, he wrote, "then it is *rational* to sanction radical acts by the US security state that, in more peaceful and normal times, would be unthinkable."[10] In this regard, consider that the Department of Homeland Security issued a terrorism advisory bulletin early in 2022 that warned about a "heightened threat environment" due to the "proliferation of false or misleading narratives, which sow discord or undermine public trust in U.S. government institutions."[11] Taken at face value, it would seem there are criticisms we cannot make about our government and narratives that are forbidden despite the First Amendment.

---

[9] Roger Kimball, "The January 6 Insurrection Hoax," *Imprimis* 50, no. 10 (October 2021), https://imprimis.hillsdale.edu/january-6-insurrection-hoax/.

[10] Glenn Greenwald, "The Histrionics and Melodrama Around 1/6 Are Laughable, but They Serve Several Key Purposes," *Glenn Greenwald* (blog), January 6, 2022, https://greenwald.substack.com/p/the-histrionics-and-melodrama-around.

[11] U.S. Department of Homeland Security, "Summary of Terrorism Threat to the U.S. Homeland," *National Terrorism Advisory System Bulletin*, February 7, 2022, https://www.dhs.gov/ntas/advisory/national-terrorism-advisory-system-bulletin-february-07-2022.

For present purposes, the issue here is not which side is right in their description of the January 6 events, but that such a deep divide over the meaning of the Capitol attack should open so quickly, and with such an air of inevitability. It was as if some potent, unseen force was pulling Americans into opposing camps, and not just in relation to the Capitol attack but across any number of major public issues that have been roiling our politics recently: the impeachments of Donald Trump, the rules surrounding our elections and their legitimacy, the public response to the COVID-19 pandemic, cancel culture and free speech, immigration, and much more. There are battle lines being drawn, as a protest song from another era put it. Political tensions are high enough that commentators have been comparing our moment to the situation prior to the Civil War. While that comparison might not be exactly apt, the stress in our public sphere is real and any path to national reconciliation is hard to imagine.

This question of reconciliation is a crucial one and can be seen in a constitutional light. This is so because in our constitutional order the people are considered sovereign and when the sovereign is divided against itself, real dangers inevitably follow. Such a division is inherently unstable and competing factions will inevitably try to subjugate one another. To Thomas Hobbes, the notion that *"sovereign power can be divided* is absolutely fatal to commonwealths."[12] But at present our sovereign, the people themselves, seems to be just that—divided.

Pluralism and the Constitution
We might, perhaps, take heart. Dealing with social and political division is in fact nothing new for our constitutional system, which

---

[12] Thomas Hobbes, *Leviathan* (Cambridge University Press, 1991), 135.

has generally proven effective at the job. Actually, conflict and strife are unavoidable facts of political life and one essential task facing every political state is to reconcile opposing views to establish some acceptable order. Different constitutional systems deal with this brute fact in various ways, including the violent suppression of dissenting elements; but all must face it.

Our constitutional system, of course, depends far more on building consensus around political goals, generally limited ones, than on simple suppression of opponents. But finding or creating that consensus in a nation that now includes 330 million people from every conceivable racial, religious, ethnic, economic, and ideological background is a massive challenge, and we can hardly take success for granted. Whether our constitutional order can withstand our current divisiveness and the mounting pressures of simmering, divided public opinion is a reasonable question.

To answer, it helps to recall some basics of American civics, especially those that relate to the challenge of reconciling factions and maintaining peace in the land. What follows are a few thoughts about how our constitutional system functions in this regard.

Liberalism and the Constitution

The first thing to say about the American political system is that it is *liberal*, and, in fact, the founding of the United States was one of the landmark events in the history of liberalism. But the word *liberal*, a key one for this book, must be understood in a particular sense. This means leaving aside its polemical uses and looking to the term's deeper historical significance. Liberalism should be seen, first, as a decisive step away from the order that characterized medieval

Europe.[13] That earlier society understood itself as a manifestation of a coherent universe, created by God, in which government, like all of creation, was part of an intelligible order. In it, all things had their place: kings, ordained by God, had theirs, which differed from that of the aristocracy, which in turn differed from that of the clergy, and so on. Each class had its niche in the system, and this order was reflected in the rights and powers of these social classes. Of course, it was also hoped that the laws in general would be attuned to the natural rights and wrongs engrained in the cosmos.

This political view came apart in the violence of the sixteenth and seventeenth centuries, and liberalism emerged out of its dissolution. One of its chief characteristics was a certain metaphysical modesty. Liberal government was *not* seen to reflect a particular divine order, and this resistance to any preordained order has been the key element of liberal DNA ever since. Rather than resting on a given cosmic order, liberals see government as a human creation, originating in the will of the people, with its direction determined by the interests of its citizenry. As for finding this direction, representative legislatures were central institutions, and it is worth noting that in the United States, at least, there are no ideological or religious restrictions on who can be elected to the legislatures. No views are ruled out a priori among candidates for office.

---

[13] Putting the matter—liberalism vs. medieval order—this starkly is useful, but the actual history behind this pivotal change is complex and liberalism itself had roots in medieval law and philosophy. To take just one example, historian Brian Tierney, pointing to the divide between Church and state, a foundation of liberal governance and present much earlier than the 17th century, wrote that "[T]he very existence of two power structures competing for men's allegiance instead of only one compelling obedience greatly enhanced the possibilities for human freedom." Brian Tierney, *The Crisis of Church and State 1050–1300* (Toronto, 1998), 2.

At the same time, liberalism also emphasized the rights of the individual, rights protected against the threat posed by overly aggressive government, including the threat of legislation passed by the individual's own representatives. In keeping with its fundamental principles, liberal government tended to be concerned with establishing liberties and protecting people against potential harms, rather than fostering any particular order. In summing up its constitutional disposition, political philosopher John Gray wrote that liberal government aimed at a "society of free men, equal under the rule of law, bound together by no common purpose, but sharing a respect for each others' rights."[14]

This ideal translated into doctrines of limited government, with internally divided powers, and specific legal protections for individual freedoms. The United States Constitution is a prime example in each of these regards. As for reconciling a diverse people and maintaining the peace, this system depends on a somewhat counterintuitive approach—not trying too hard. With limited, liberal government, the burden of ordering society is largely dispersed among the people themselves. How does this work? Consider the Bill of Rights and, specifically, the First Amendment. The whole purpose of the bill is to limit government and to protect the broader society from its potentially invasive actions. In effect, the bill places certain rights beyond the realm of political questions altogether, so that, in the words of one Supreme Court justice, they "may not be submitted to vote; they depend on no elections."[15] Consider, here,

---

[14] John Gray, *Liberalism* (University of Minnesota Press, 1986), 12.

[15] The justice was Robert Jackson, who served on the Supreme Court 1941–1954. See his opinion in *West Virginia State Board of Education v. Barnette*, 319 U.S. 624 (1943).

the opening of the First Amendment: "Congress shall make no law.
. . .."

In the words that follow, the Amendment specifies one of those things that Congress shall make no laws about, which is "the establishment of religion or prohibiting the free exercise thereof. . . .." By ruling out the possibility of establishing a national religion, the First Amendment removes from politics the contentious question of which religion will reign in the land. It leaves the question of religious adherence to the people in their private lives. This cannot end all political friction generated by religious issues, nor can moral questions ever be separated from politics. Thus, difficult challenges relating to religion in public life remain. But the United States has likely saved itself a good deal of trouble over its history by preventing the establishment of a single, favored national church. Perhaps as a result, our fantastically diverse nation has managed to live with a good deal of religious conviction among its citizens, but at the same time with relatively little religious repression or violent sectarian strife.

We find a parallel phenomenon if we turn to a different field, that of the economy. Historically, our constitutional order has left the citizenry relatively free to pursue their interests as they see fit, in relatively free markets. We should not underestimate the potential for conflict in this sphere of life. Economic activity necessarily brings people with opposed interests into tight relationships. Sellers, for instance, generally want to get high prices for the goods and services they offer, while buyers want to keep those prices low. And this rule permeates the economy, not only in wholesale and retail trade, but between renters and landlords, workers and employers, and so forth.

By standing mostly aside, a limited government lets the burden of reconciling these differing interests fall to private citizens and the myriad choices they make in the course of daily life. And here, as with religious freedom, the results have been positive, though surely far from perfect. Relatively free of direction imposed from above, the American economy grew over time into an extremely complex, refined, and productive system. While its rewards are spread very unequally and poverty is still very much a reality, material abundance in America has been the rule. And despite the potential conflicts inherent in a competitive system, our economic life has been and remains mostly peaceful; though, again, there have certainly been exceptions.[16]

Limits on "Limited" Government
While the liberal interpretation of the constitution system tells a very real story, it is, at the same time, only a partial telling. What it leaves out are the various ways in which the American political system never was perfectly liberal and the ways in which the need (and desire) for order has asserted itself since the founding. Indeed, the founding itself provides an example. Had American leaders at that time really wanted a government with very limited powers, we might have retained the Articles of Confederation. This agreement among the young states of America established less of an actual national government and more "a firm league of friendship," as the document itself puts it, and its terms made governmental action at the national level difficult indeed.

---

[16] I am thinking here especially of the occasional violence related to the growth of the labor movement and its attempted suppression.

As a result, however, problems accumulated after independence
that seemed insoluble without some more effective, centralized
power. Those problems included a complex debt crisis, dysfunc-
tional trade laws, and weak infrastructure. It was governmental
infirmity in the face of these troubles that led to the conclusion that
America needed a new constitution in the first place. In *Federalist*
no. 1, Alexander Hamilton, having noted the "inefficiency of the
subsisting federal government," called for a new government "ener-
getic" enough to insure "political prosperity." As events unfolded,
Hamilton's vision carried the day and the new Constitution was
adopted despite a determined, articulate opposition. Moreover, its
powers were soon put to various uses, which included founding a
national bank, establishing tariffs to protect America's budding
manufacturing sector, and setting financial policies to tame the debt
problem.

It was not just in economic matters that the ideal of limited
government was itself limited in the early republic. State legislatures
passed many laws designed to impose a degree of moral or social
order on the citizenry. Of course, there were laws against murder,
robbery, physical attacks, and such. But there were also laws that
provided state support for religion, such as those in Connecticut,
where Congregationalism was the state's established church until
1818.[17] Remember, at the time the First Amendment applied only
to the national legislature ("Congress shall pass no law . . . ."), and
not to state laws. A number of states also had blasphemy laws,
including New York, which prosecuted one John Ruggles for the

---

[17] Curtis W. Freeman, "The Wall of Separation," *Christian History*, https://
christianhistoryinstitute.org/magazine/article/baptist-liberties-and-the-
wall-of-separation.

crime. In a tavern Ruggles had said in a loud voice, "Jesus Christ was a bastard and his mother must be a whore." Arrested, tried, and found guilty, Ruggles appealed his conviction, and subsequently the case went before New York's Supreme Court of Judicature. In 1811 the court upheld the conviction. Its decision, written by the highly regarded Justice James Kent, denied that blasphemy laws violated the First Amendment ban on established religion,[18] and noted that offenses against religion, such as blasphemy, were punishable because "they strike at the root of moral obligation, and weaken the security of the social ties. We stand equally in need, now as formerly, of all that moral discipline, and of those principles of virtue, which help to bind society together."

It is worth noting that Justice Kent's reasoning is inconsistent with John Gray's distillation of liberalism, in which a "society of free men" would be "bound together by no common purpose." But the New York court's acceptance of blasphemy laws and similar morality-based legislation does not prove that the United States was actually illiberal so much as it suggests that there were tensions between its liberal and less liberal features. American political society was one in which the people determined the laws by which it would live. And it is only natural, given a reasonably coherent culture, that its people would encourage certain behaviors while discouraging others and use the law to do so.

---

[18] Kent wrote in *People v. Ruggles*: "Though the constitution has discarded religious establishments, it does not forbid judicial cognizance [sic] of those offences against religion and morality which have no reference to such establishment, or to any particular form of government, but are punishable because they strike at the root of moral obligation, and weaken the security of the social ties." See *The Founders' Constitution*, vol. 5, eds. Philip B. Kurland and Ralph Lerner (Liberty Fund, 1987), 102.

The Constitution Today: Two Perspectives

The tension between liberty and order under the Constitution has been there since the beginning and remains in place today, as it must. A society living without any order is no society at all; nor can people live without some sense of freedom and personal agency. How to find a fruitful balance between the two is a key constitutional question for any state or nation, but is a particular challenge for a nation as vast and diverse as ours. The hope is that the Constitution provides a framework, somewhat flexible, under which the American people can accomplish the feat.

Whether that hope is realistic or not is a question we must face in our intensely polarized time. Perhaps the challenge in finding an acceptable type and level of order is particularly challenging at present, given those deep divides. And while public figures love to pay homage to the Constitution, people on opposing political sides might well feel as if the American constitutional system is in fact failing and might even be irredeemable.

Progressives

Consider the position of contemporary progressives, who believe in nothing so much as the need to make progress in solving the problems we face. Inevitably, this brings progressives into conflict with the liberal aspects of American constitutionalism. To achieve progressive ends means acting on notions of order, both in determining what is right to do and in mustering the power necessary to achieve those goals. For example, a chief progressive concern presently is the threat of climate change and their main weapon to reduce the threat is cutting carbon dioxide emissions. Climate change is not a minor issue, but, as many progressives believe, an existential danger. It was also a plank in the Democratic party's 2020 platform. "Climate change is a global emergency . . . the United States—and the world—must achieve net-zero greenhouse gas emissions as soon as possible, and no later than 2050," the platform reads. In addition, the party is committed "to eliminating carbon pollution from power plants by 2035."[19]

Whatever one thinks about the threat of climate change, one must understand that reordering the American energy system on this scale is an extraordinarily ambitious goal. The current energy system is immensely complex, involving exploration, extraction, refining, and distribution of fossil fuels for use in homes, businesses, and transportation. It is not too much to say that our lives are dependent on these fuels. In terms of technology and infrastructure, building a parallel system based on alternative sources that would accomplish the Democratic Party's goals would be a herculean task.

But the political challenge is daunting as well, which is where constitutional matters enter in. To set major policy directions we pass laws. But the framers of the Constitution made it difficult to pass laws, the better to prevent overly aggressive or invasive government. To become law, a bill has to pass both the House of Representatives and the Senate, then be signed by the president, and finally pass constitutional muster in the courts if challenged legally. In Congress, where members represent every corner of the nation and a correspondingly wide range of interests, there are any number of ways to weaken or kill a bill as it makes its way through the

---

[19] Democratic National Committee, "Combating the Climate Crisis and Pursuing Environmental Justice," https://democrats.org/where-we-stand/party-platform/combating-the-climate-crisis-and-pursuing-environmental-justice/.

complex legislative process. In the case of cutting fossil fuel use, vested interests, including millions of families who depend on jobs in the energy sector, have a stake in maintaining our current energy system. They will not sacrifice their livelihoods lightly. Democratic talking points might stress the employment opportunities that will blossom in the solar or wind power industries as the energy switch takes hold, but for those in Appalachia's coal country or the Texas oil patch, those claims are cold comfort.

More to the political point, those who depend on the current energy system for their livelihood will have their say in Congress, given our constitutional system, and their representatives will have real power to derail any transition to a new energy regime. Even if proponents of a green conversion actually had a majority in the House of Representatives, the Senate would likely be a sticking point for any legislation with teeth enough to actually bring about significant change. To the degree one considers carbon reduction the only way to avert disaster, the American constitutional system itself must be seen as a serious problem.

The Democratic Party is, again, on record as supporting the remaking of the massive energy sector, an effort it believes is crucial to well-being of the planet. At the same time, constitutional provisions make legislation to accomplish this extremely difficult to enact. This must lead to grave constitutional frustration among progressives, and in fact they have been so vexed since the origins of their movement. Woodrow Wilson shared this frustration when, as a political scientist in academia, he asked the question: How can one accomplish big, necessary things within a system that doesn't naturally do them? The answer, from the aggrieved Wilson, was that the Constitution itself must evolve or die. It should be seen less through the lens of Newtonian physics, as if it were a perfect, changeless machine, and more in terms of evolution: "Living political constitutions must be Darwinian in structure and in practice. Society is a living organism and must obey the laws of life, not of mechanics; it must develop."[20]

Though Wilson's hoped-for evolution did come to pass,[21] progressives' underlying frustrations with the American system have remained. Professors Ryan Doerfler (Harvard Law School) and Samuel Moyn (Yale Law School) expressed this in a 2022 *New York Times* op-ed titled "The Constitution Is Broken and Should Not Be Reclaimed."[22] Indeed, their trouble with the system is such that they question the value of having any constitution whatsoever. By their nature, constitutions impose a higher law by which any legislation must be judged. In doing so, they "inevitably orient us to the past and misdirect the present into a dispute over what people agreed on once upon a time, not on what the present and future demand for and from those who live now." Thus, constitutions are inherently conservative, preventing flexibility in responding to current challenges.

This is clearly the case, Doerfler and Moyn argue, with the various anti-democratic elements of the U.S. Constitution—they cite the Electoral College and the Senate in this regard—which act

---

[20] "Woodrow Wilson: The New Freedom, 1913," National Constitution Center, https://constitutioncenter.org/the-constitution/historic-document-library/detail/woodrow-wilson-the-new-freedom-1913.

[21] This evolution of the Constitution, or our understanding of it, will be explored much more fully in subsequent chapters.

[22] Ryan Doerfler and Samuel Moyn, "The Constitution Is Broken and Should Not Be Reclaimed," *The New York Times*, April 9, 2022.

as "impediments to redistributive change. . . ." Better, in their eyes, would be a regime in which majoritarian, democratic forces could prevail and shape the destiny of the nation without being hostage to archaic restraints. So, for example, we might vote for presidents directly, without the Electoral College. Similarly, we could reorganize Congress so that the Senate might retain some power to revise laws but lose its power to obstruct them. By taking such steps, Doerfler and Moyn aim to build a system where we might "engage in the constant reinvention of our society under our own power, without the illusion that the past stands in the way."

Conservatives

If Woodrow Wilson and his progressive heirs face constitutional headaches, so too do conservative Americans. First, however, it will help to define *conservatism*, since the term is used in so many different ways and contexts. For the purposes of this book, the words of the late English philosopher Roger Scruton will serve: "[C]onservatism arises directly from the sense that one belongs to some continuing and pre-existing social order and that this fact is all-important in determining what to do."[23]

For American conservatives, however, this definition raises difficulties, not least in deciding what is their highest priority when it comes to conserving things. If the all-important fact is a preexisting social order, as Scruton suggests, does that social order trump the Constitution itself? For some conservatives at least, the answer is yes, and the document itself should be seen as dependent on a

---

[23] Roger Scruton, *The Meaning of Conservatism* (St. Augustine's Press, 2002), 10.

more fundamental "constitution," that is the habits, values, mores, and conventions of the people.

As conservative legal scholars point out, the Constitution itself grew out of such soil, and the pre-existing culture of the American people was reflected in the work of its authors. Moreover, when their work was done, the Constitution was submitted to the people, state by state, for their approval. Into the debates over ratification, Americans brought all their values and commitments, and engaged in an intense, prolonged discussion about the country's political future. The legitimacy of the new Constitution depended on the people's consent, and in turn on the order that shaped the people themselves.

The ratification of the Constitution through this process offered concrete proof that it was in tune with some critical mass of the people. Succeeding decades reinforced the notion. Under the Constitution, Americans generally prospered, economically and otherwise. Through its long-term success, the Constitution earned a strong measure of popular support, which eventually developed into a kind or reverence.[24] Early in the twentieth century prominent New York attorney Henry Estabrook paid tribute to the US Constitution in these terms: "Our great and sacred Constitution, serene and inviolable, stretches its beneficent powers over our land . . . like the outstretched arm of God himself. . . . Oh Marvelous Constitution! Magic Parchment! . . . Maker, Monitor, Guardian of Mankind!"[25]

---

[24] Southern secession and the Civil War amount to the greatest exceptions.

[25] Alexander M. Bickel, *The Supreme Court and the Idea of Progress* (Yale University Press, 1978), 15.

Thus the mystique of the Constitution became a part of the Scrutonian "pre-existing social order" of the United States, and its veneration one of our norms. But this cannot obscure the fact that the Constitution is also rooted in liberal thought, which meant that it was, and would always be, in tension with conservative values. For example, the liberalism of the American system set the stage for a dynamic economic system that has proved revolutionary, reshaping society in profound ways.

Just as importantly, the liberal aspects of American constitutionalism have acted as a solvent of traditional order in other, non-economic ways. Consider the free speech/flag-burning case, *Texas v. Johnson*, decided by the United States Supreme Court in 1989. Gregory Lee Johnson, a young radical, burned an American flag as part of a political protest in Dallas, Texas during the Republican Convention of1984. Texas, however, had a law on its books that banned the desecration of the flag. Thus, Johnson was arrested, tried, and sentenced for the crime. He appealed the conviction, claiming that flag burning in his case was a form of political speech, and thus protected under the First Amendment.

The Supreme Court sided with Johnson, agreeing that the right of free speech extended far enough to cover "expressive conduct," including the burning of the flag. In line with a basic premise of liberal government, the court refused to rule Johnson's political views out of bounds, nor his means of promoting them.

But it is worth looking at Justice William Rehnquist's dissent to understand the court's decision in context. To start, Rehnquist notes the flag's profound symbolic meaning for millions of Americans, as well as its obvious status as official emblem of the nation. All this points to the "uniquely deep awe and respect" for the flag among the American people, for many of whom its burning must always be a gross insult. Continuing, Rehnquist points out that one of the essential purposes of a democracy is to "legislate against conduct that is regarded as evil and profoundly offensive to the majority of the people—whether it be murder, embezzlement, pollution or flagburning [*sic*]."[26]

This was the heart of the dissent, but, as we know, the majority held otherwise. Written by Justice William Brennan, the majority opinion makes the point that the central idea behind the First Amendment is that "government may not prohibit the expression of an idea simply because society finds the idea itself offensive or disagreeable." In addition, the decision restates from an earlier decision the following: "If there is any fixed star in our constitutional constellation, it is that no official, high or petty, can prescribe what shall be orthodox in politics, nationalism, religion, or other matters of opinion, or forces citizens to confess by word or act their faith therein."[27]

Thus the liberal logic embedded in the Constitution overcame the claims of, essentially, the sense of good order held by Texans, as codified by their laws. Moreover, the *Texas v. Johnson* case is hardly alone as an example of this dynamic, in which liberal values override those of some concrete, popular order. Conservatives can claim that the law is being misinterpreted when the liberal logic wins in legal battle, but those outcomes can hardly be thought of as outside the mainstream of American constitutional understanding.

---

[26] Texas v. Johnson, 491, U.S. 397 (1989).

[27] Texas v. Johnson, 491, U.S. 397 (1989).

Our Constitutional Order: Three Views

That the Constitution manages to frustrate both conservatives and progressives at times might be a source of its strength. By making it difficult for any faction to dominate, American government is less prone to the abuses we associate with authoritarian regimes. The political balances institutionalized under the Constitution earn a measure of devotion from both sides, thus making sure that relatively few people are left without any stake in the system.

But the document is not magical, and there is a danger that a decisive percentage of the people will grow frustrated enough with the constitutional system that its support slips beneath some necessary level. And there are worrying signs that faith in the system is failing, with barely two in ten Americans believing that government does the right thing "'just about always' (2 percent) or 'most of the time' (21 percent)."[28]

In any case, the constitutional tensions outlined above will be explored in greater depth in the chapters that follow. The text will touch on major constitutional themes, including the tensions between freedom and order, but also changes in the way the Constitution has been understood over time, the migration of power among the branches of government, the balance of power between government and the private sector, as well as the fundamental source of government's legitimacy. To see the state of our constitutional health as clearly as possible, these chapters explore the differing perspectives of three prominent legal scholars who hold strongly contrasting views: Richard A. Epstein, Cass Sunstein, and

---

[28] "Public Trust in Government, 1958-2024," Pew Research Center, June 24, 2024, https://www.pewresearch.org/politics/2024/06/24/public-trust-in-government-1958-2024/.

Adrian Vermeule. I do not try to compare their views in a formulaic, point-by-point manner, though the content of their views offers plenty of opportunity for comparison. Instead, the chapters let each scholar speak for himself, allowing his interests, concerns, and constitutional positions to stand on their own.

Nor do I try to reconcile their views to find some promising synthesis of my own (which, given their differences, would be somewhere between difficult and impossible), or try to prove one's superiority over the others. A central purpose of this book runs directly counter to any such effort. We need to understand that the political and even constitutional differences in this country run deep, not only through the people at large but among its best legal thinkers. We would be mistaken in hoping that our divisions might be healed by simply looking to some constitutional expert for an authoritative, disinterested view to put our disagreements to rest. What will help is to clarify our current political impasse, see how it grew out of constitutional choices made over time, and consider the directions we might take in the effort to move toward a more fruitful, satisfactory political future.

Chapter 1

A CLASSICAL LIBERAL
TAKES STOCK

To put our current constitutional discontent into perspective, one must take a look back and follow the steps that brought us to this point. One scholar who has paid close attention to this progression is Richard A. Epstein, author of more than fifteen books and dozens of law review and other articles. He has not only been prolific, but has also been one of the most influential of contemporary legal thinkers.[1] As an undergraduate, his strong record at Columbia earned him a Kellett Fellowship, which provided the opportunity to study law at Oxford. There he was immersed in the English common law tradition, which would mark his later scholarship. After law school and a stint at the University of Southern

---

[1] "Celebrating Richard Epstein," *The University of Chicago Law School News*, April 19, 2018, https://www.law.uchicago.edu/news/celebrating-richard-epstein, for more biographical background see also Jennifer S. Frey, "Introducing Richard Epstein," *NYU School of Law Magazine*, http://magazine.law.nyu.edu/index.html%3Fp=1045.html.

California, Epstein landed at the University of Chicago, well known for the strong economic focus of its legal scholars, and this too had a profound effect on his thinking. Epstein taught at Chicago for thirty-eight years and more recently has been on the faculty at New York University.

More Basics of Liberal Government

Many observers describe Epstein as a libertarian, as he sometimes does himself, but a more precise term for his views is *classical liberal*. What makes his views classical is his looking back to the period when political liberalism was first taking shape and its essentials being defined. As noted earlier, liberal government emerged as the medieval order waned. In taking definite form, liberal theorists reimagined the whole foundation on which government might rest, setting the stage for an epochal shift. If we want a return to good constitutional health, Epstein believes, it is useful to look back to the original understanding of liberal government as it crystallized and when its doctrines were especially clear.

John Locke and the Social Contract

As liberal political theory was forming and its key thinkers searched for those new foundations, they found it useful to produce what was, in effect, a new creation myth about the origins of government. The result was social contract theory. Different thinkers offered different variations on the theme, but these retellings shared a basic structure: Once humans lived freely in a state of nature prior to any government. In time they found it useful or necessary to join together and form a government, the better to live secure, fruitful lives. By entering into this social contract, people traded away some of their natural freedom for the benefits that government can bring. For philosophers, telling this story—*thought experiment* might be a better term—allowed them to explore beliefs about political fundamentals, including the relationship between the individual and society, and the essential purposes of government.

But how one imagined the state of nature and the social contract had important ramifications. Consider the story according to Thomas Hobbes, one of the great seventeenth century theorists who made use of the theory. For Hobbes, the state of nature amounted to a "war of all against all," as self-interested individuals endlessly threatened each other in a competition for scarce goods. To counter this grim condition, in which life was "solitary, poor, nasty, brutish and short," Hobbes imagined a government endowed with absolute sovereign power: a Leviathan able to control the destructive inclinations of human nature.

Another social contract theorist, John Locke, had a different, sunnier take on the state of nature, one that Richard Epstein embraces and that tracks more closely with the US Constitution.[2] In Locke's description, the threat to life and possessions came not from all sides, but from a relatively few plunderers. Apart from them, people tended to live in a degree of harmony and according to reason. Since the threat to individuals in this scenario is less pervasive than in Hobbes's imagined state of nature, Locke saw less need for an absolute sovereign to rule over us. Instead, a limited

---

[2] For Epstein's take on Locke, see Richard A. Epstein, *Takings* (Harvard University Press, 1985), 9–16; reviewing Locke's thought will also provide a useful touchstone in the subsequent chapters of this book, on Cass Sunstein and Adrian Vermeule.

government would suffice, one that left the balance of the people's natural freedom in place.

In this version of the social contract, Locke emphasized that freedom was a gift of nature, as was, in a related way, the right to property. Not only could people live as they chose in nature, they could also claim from its bounty whatever resources they found in order to feed, clothe, and shelter themselves and their families. Moreover, they had the right to defend their gains in property against those who would transgress these primordial rights. In this scenario, the social contract is joined in order to protect both the freedoms of the people and the property they accumulate.

Though people, as Locke imagined them, are not naturally rapacious, they do possess a strong instinct for self-interest, an instinct that Epstein has no interest in denying. People are naturally oriented to work for their own benefit and the support of those closest to them, and any form of government that fails to take this self-interest into account misses an essential element of human nature and is doomed to fail. At the same time, however, experience shows that seeking one's own betterment is not simply a zero-sum competition with others. Rather, Locke's vision of human self-interest also saw humans as naturally cooperative. Left to their own devices, people will join forces in the effort to develop resources and improve their lives. The incentive to cooperate is just as strong as the instinct for self-interest, and is, indeed, another facet of that instinct. Moreover, the drive to improve one's lot increases the productivity of society as a whole. Thus, suppressing self-interest is not only a transgression against nature, but also, somewhat para-doxically, a danger to social well-being.

Many essentials of liberal government find their basis in Locke's theories. Rights and liberties are rooted in the natural order, for example, and are the birthright of all people, equally. The protection of property, a key motive for the social contract itself, is an essential responsibility of government. In keeping with this responsibility, government rightly provides for domestic security, a legal system to settle disputes, and other necessities that people must have to flourish but cannot supply effectively through private action alone.[3] But Locke's philosophy also leads to the presumption of strongly limited government: If people agree to yield some rights in exchange for a more secure and stable society, they remain free by nature and government has no right to trespass on personal liberties without necessary cause. In addition, we see in Locke the idea that governmental legitimacy is based on the consent of the governed. Government is essentially a contract with the people and if government fails to meet its obligations, the contract is void. More subtly perhaps, there is also a presumption as well that, while people are social, the individual (or the family) is primary and social associations beyond that are voluntary. Of course, the importance of Locke's social contract is not that the myth itself is historically accurate, but that governance that follows Lockean principles resonates with human nature. As classical liberals see things, it works.

---

[3] The key difference between classical liberals and libertarians comes here, with libertarians being much less willing to accept the legitimate role of government in such matters. As Epstein put it, "The fatal weakness of modern hard-line libertarian views, such as those advanced by the late Robert Nozick, is that they cannot explain how states rightly gain legitimacy and the resources to prevent violence, enforce contractual promises, and supply needed infrastructure." See Richard A. Epstein, *The Classical Liberal Constitution* (Harvard University Press, 2014), 20.

All of these fundamental beliefs shape liberal government, very much including the constitutional system of the United States. And both Locke and the US Constitution are foundational to Richard Epstein's legal thought.

The Classical Liberal and Social Norms

Lockean liberalism entails strictly limited government, but this is hardly the same thing as embracing an ungoverned or unruly society. Social order can be propagated through means apart from the strictly legal, which brings us to the subject of *social norms*. This is an area to which Richard Epstein pays close attention and where, unlike governmental regulation, he is more bullish than bearish. Social norms are the conventions, mores, habits, and values that guide people in the myriad judgments they make daily. These judgments, taken together, reward some behaviors and discourage others, and in doing so act as a sort of extra-official mode of government.

Richard Epstein writes sympathetically about social norms as a key part of the way we foster order in society. Comparing social norms to the legal approach for enforcing standards, he writes: "Bone does not always rub against bone; sometimes cartilage softens the impact."[4] But while social norms might be more forgiving in some respects than the law, their violation brings undeniable penalties, including ostracism and a loss of status or reputation. One can imagine, for example, a person who chooses to get especially garish tattoos that might turn off potential employers, and in doing so loses many job opportunities.

---

[4] Richard A. Epstein, *Principles of a Free Society* (Perseus Publishing, 1998), 46.

While it might be tempting to pass over social norms in thinking about legal and constitutional matters, this is a mistake in Epstein's eyes. In his 1998 book, *Principles for a Free Society: Reconciling Individual Liberty with the Common Good*, Epstein acknowledges the crucial role norms play as well as their power: "Reputation is [now] explicitly recognized for what it always has been—a powerful constraint on human behavior. In addition, other forms of social sanction, ranging from simple disapproval and gossip to ostracism and exclusion, can be directed in predictable ways at antisocial forms of conduct."[5] Relatively strong social norms have strengths that law cannot match. Where law is, by its nature, rigid and centralized, social norms are responsive to diffuse needs and interests. Thus, they do not reflect centralized planning and are less prone to "partisan manipulating," as Epstein notes.[6]

Of course, even strong social norms do not render law unnecessary. Legal remedies are often necessary to protect the innocent and promote good order. It is also the case that social norms, despite evolving out of practical experience and being guided by an instinct for positive outcomes,[7] can themselves bring about bad results. "[W]hatever the working presumption, nothing in principle guarantees that any social norm generated by a social group must necessarily be regarded as good."[8] The social conventions that supported

---

[5] Epstein, *Principles*, 47.

[6] Epstein, *Principles*, 48.

[7] About social norms, Epstein writes "diffuse and decentralized origin becomes an advantage, suggesting that the durability of a norm is attributable to the way in which it uniformly advances the interest of group members." See Epstein, *Principles*, 48.

[8] Epstein, *Principles*, 49.

racial discrimination in the twentieth century provide an example where norms failed and legal redress was required.

Epstein, however, worries that the balance between social norms and laws has shifted too strongly toward the legal side of the ledger. One simple concern with this proliferation is that law is expensive to produce and enforce.[9] More subtly, however, when too much of a society's intercourse is managed through law, it changes the ecology in which we act. Over-legalization makes our responsibilities to others more formal than they would be otherwise and can decrease the immediate sense of personal responsibility. In many cases, Epstein says, "legal intervention weakens social sanctions that have operated well outside the glare of the law."[10]

Epstein uses an example from his own life to illustrate. In 1972, as a young academic, he moved to Chicago, where he and his wife needed an apartment. At one promising location he read the lease and found that the landlord assumed no obligation for repairs in the rental units. At the same time, however, Epstein knew that the landlord kept a maintenance crew on call to make repairs when necessary. This made him wonder: Why the tough stance in the lease when the repair policy was generous in practice? The answer had everything to do with social norms. By not agreeing upfront to fix everything, the landlord placed responsibility on renters to take care of their apartment. At the same time, by keeping maintenance up to a high standard, the landlord earned a strong reputation among potential renters and he was able to sift applicants for those who appeared most reliable.

---

[9] Richard A. Epstein, *Simple Rules for a Complex World* (Harvard University Press, 1995), 6–8.

[10] Epstein, *Principles*, 58.

Had the landlord specified in a contract that he would repair damages as a rule, it would have set the relationship on more rigid grounds. Instead, he preferred to rely on more informal and supple relationships and, as Epstein notes, the approach worked well. His own experience with the apartment was highly satisfactory and the landlord's business prospered for decades. A reliance on law might seem to promise power over bad behaviors, in this case and others. But it is often best, Epstein believes, to resist the over-legalizing of our social life. "The constant pressure to convert social norms to legal norms does not serve to rectify some imperfections; rather, it gets rid of small imperfections and replaces them with a larger one."[11]

Government, Limited and Legitimate

Having covered some of the basics that inform Richard Epstein's constitutional thought, it is time to focus on how his vision applies in more specific ways. These specifics emphasize the principles that establish clear limits on governmental action as well as those that legitimize such action.

The Police Power

For starters, there is the acceptable authorization for government action known as *the police power.* The term is somewhat indefinite, but in a common formulation, the police power justifies a government's regulation of behaviors that endanger the health, safety, morals, or general welfare of the people. Given the breadth of this definition, one could say that the police power is

---

[11] Epstein, *Principles*, 64.

assumed in virtually all government, being something like the *ur*-rationale for state action. It justifies laws to protect the well-being of the people, and in doing so often infringes on personal freedom. Think of state laws against the use of recreational drugs, for example.

Though the term does not appear in the Constitution, it is a prominent feature of the common law, both in the United States and in the English tradition. The police power naturally provides the basis for a good deal of legislation. In this country, the states, rather than the nation, have historically held much of the power to enact statutes grounded in the police powers. This division of labor is reinforced by the words of the Tenth Amendment: "[T]he powers not delegated to the Federal Government are reserved to the states or to the people." In state law, we see the police powers applied in all sorts of ways: state laws banning prostitution or gambling, enforcing lockdowns during the COVID-19 pandemic, or protecting wetlands with environmental laws.

Thus the police powers could be used to justify an exceedingly wide array of state actions, an open-endedness that Epstein finds worrisome. So the question arises: How are the police powers, which are legitimate, applied in ways that are consistent with liberal, limited government?

Textual Interpretation

Epstein starts by making the general point that, though the police powers are not mentioned in the Constitution, their application must be consistent with it—government should not be in the business of enacting laws that violate the terms of the Constitution. To police the police power, start by interpreting the Constitution rightly.

Doing so is a challenge, but we can begin by simply reading its text. Start from a "blank slate," Epstein says, to get a "proper understanding . . . in its original written form, unadorned by previous interpretive efforts."[12] This first step in constitutional interpretation must "rely largely on the public meaning" of the language. Constitutional text is somewhat specialized, but not hermetic, not the property of some priestly class. The interpretation of a constitution's terms must fit with the general understandings held by the people themselves.

However, while some passages from the US Constitution can hardly be construed in more than one way—the rule about presidents being at least thirty-five years old, for instance—others demand further explanation. What does "due process of law" mean, for example, when it must be applied in a wide variety of circumstances? Thus the necessary second step is to construe texts as they are applied to actual problems.

So the great challenge of constitutional interpretation is finding a way to balance two demands: faithfulness to the meaning of the text as written and creative application of that meaning to concrete disputes. For Epstein, the best way to navigate this challenge is to understand the Constitution as a coherent, carefully constructed whole, best understood as advancing the ideals of classical liberalism.[13] So, when interpreting the extent of the police powers, jurists should tend toward a narrow construal rather than an expansive one that gives government greater leeway in regulating people's

---

[12] Epstein, *The Classical Liberal Constitution* (Harvard University Press, 2014), 45.

[13] Epstein, *The Classical Liberal Constitution*, 71.

choices. This is so because the thrust of the Constitution as a whole points this way, toward strictly limited government.

An example will help here. Consider the crucial concept of the "general welfare," one of the areas where the police power applies. The phrase also appears in the Constitution, crucially in the "Spending Clause," Article 1, Section 8, which reads as follows:

> The Congress shall have Power To lay and collect Taxes, Duties, Imposts and Excises, to pay the Debts and provide for the common Defense and general Welfare of the United States. . . .

Given that the term helps define Congress's power and is thus highly important, how should the "general Welfare" be understood? It can be read in more than one way. In a 2012 Supreme Court decision, Justice Ruth Bader Ginsburg gave it an open-ended interpretation: "Congress has broad authority to construct and adjust spending programs to meet its contemporary understanding of 'the general Welfare.'"[14] If the phrase's meaning is limited mainly by what Congress chooses to spend money on, in principle there might not be any limit to "the general Welfare" at all.

For Epstein, such a relaxed reading of the clause, though widely accepted, is inconsistent with the basic purpose of the Constitution and wrong. In his view, rather than being treated as a broad authorization to spend as Congress wishes, the general welfare clause should be read as a limitation. Tax dollars should

---

[14] National Federation of Independent Business v. Sebellius, 132 U.S. 2658, 2012. See also Epstein, *The Classical Liberal Constitution*, 195.

be spent *only* in ways that benefit the people generally, for example, and not some subset of the population, geographic, demographic, or otherwise. So one criterion for federal programs is that they must not exclude anyone by design. In Epstein's eyes, this should apply to all sorts of government programs, such as price supports for the dairy industry, where a strict reading might well delegitimize them. In this way, interpreting the phrase "general welfare" in tune with the meaning of the Constitution as a whole yields a classically liberal result.

Eminent Domain

If the police power underwrites government action in given cases, so too does the power of *eminent domain*. In contrast to the police power, the US Constitution is quite specific, though somewhat enigmatic, about eminent domain. Here are the words in question, the "Takings Clause" of the Fifth Amendment:

> . . . nor shall private property be taken for public use, without just compensation.

Though one has to look closely, there is an implied power in this clause that *allows* government to take property from private parties for the benefit of the broader public. If it was not legitimate to take private property for public use, why mention it at all? This power, which is of great interest to Epstein, is one he accepts as entirely legitimate. At the same time, the Constitution also places limits on this power by insisting that the state provide "just compensation" for the taking. To consider a simple case, if the government needs a piece of land in order to build a post office, it is empowered to take that property even if the owner objects. But the government must pay the owner a just amount for it.

However straightforward the takings clause appears, the devil is in the details and to Epstein the power of eminent domain is pregnant with complexities with profoundly serious implications. Here again, the brief clause quoted above can be interpreted in varying ways, ways that are either consistent with classical liberalism or that open paths to far more active government.

We can start with the term *private property*. In the case of the land needed for a post office, the property in question is real estate and just compensation fairly clear. But, as Locke and Epstein would have it, there are other forms of property, which raises questions about how just compensation might be applied. For example, to the classical liberal, property includes one's capacity to earn a living and a government regulation might limit a person's future earnings, creating a so-called *regulatory taking*. Suppose, for example, a landlord makes a living by renting apartments in a given city and plans to continue doing so. If that city imposes rent control, it might dramatically diminish the landlord's earnings. Does this intrusion on the landlord's property rights qualify as a taking? Must he or she be compensated? If so, how would one calculate that compensation?

In addition to *private property*, a second term from the takings clause requires attention, the phrase *public use*. By citing public use as a key justification for the claim of eminent domain, one can assume that the term was put there to reinforce the idea that government cannot take property for private uses. Thus, the state cannot take property to provide, say, a new home for a senator's child. Taking property for such a use amounts to the government forcing one citizen to hand over goods to another. And this would defy a basic responsibility of government, familiar from Locke, that of securing people against the infringement on their property by others.

Here, however, Epstein notes another potential flexibility in the judicial interpretation of the takings clause, once again dangerous in his eyes. He quotes from a 1984 Supreme Court decision that says that "public use" amounts to anything "rationally related to a conceivable public purpose."[15] Epstein also cites the opinion (again, wrong to Epstein) of constitutional scholar Bruce Ackerman who wrote, to a similar effect, that "any state purpose otherwise constitutional should qualify as sufficiently 'public' to justify a taking."[16]

To Epstein, this open-endedness is a troubling, though typical, failure to hold constitutional terms to their proper, principled standard. The public use clause is better understood, he argues, as having real teeth and imposing real limits on the power of eminent domain. The benefits that come from government takings should benefit the public generally and not exclude anyone. The post office built on land taken by eminent domain, for instance, serves all; no one is excluded. But applying that standard to rent control (if one considers it a taking) leads to a different conclusion. Some will benefit, but others will not, starting with landlords but not stopping there. Some people will be shut out of the rent-controlled market and forced to look for a rental property not covered by the regulation, likely at inflated rates given the realities of supply and demand.

Finally, a third phrase from the takings clause that needs scrutiny is *just compensation*. One assumes the meaning of "just" is simply

---

[15] *Hawaii Housing Authority v. Midkiff*, 467 U.S. 229 (1984).

[16] Richard Epstein, *Takings: Private Property and the Power of Eminent Domain* (Harvard University Press, 1985), 162.

"full," so, going back to the post office example, if the property taken from the private party is worth $1 million, it makes sense that the government cannot pay half that. But, as Epstein points out, the Constitution specifies only that the compensation be just, not that it take any specific form, such as money. The openness here leads to the possibility of what might be called in-kind compensation. A given regulation might cause a direct financial loss for a party, but that loss could be mitigated by the general benefits the regulation brings. That benefit can count as in-kind compensation, even if it is not, by monetary standards, full. And this interpretive looseness can again be put to questionable uses as Epstein sees it.

Consider one Supreme Court case, *Agins v. City of Tiburon*, which Epstein writes about in detail. The Agins were a couple who bought five acres of land in Tiburon, California overlooking San Francisco Bay. They had plans to build residences on the land and sell them at a later date. They ran into a complication, however, arising from pressure on the city of Tiburon to formulate a plan to protect the local environment and open spaces. With open space highly limited, the city thought about buying the Agins property from the couple and leaving it undeveloped, which would help meet their environmental obligation. And the city actually authorized spending of $1.25 million to do just that. However, city officials devised a less expensive plan to meet the same goal. Tiburon passed a rezoning plan that made it virtually impossible for the Agins to carry out their building plan. This in turn left the property undeveloped, which helped Tiburon meet its environmental objective.

This was a winning outcome for the city, but not for the Agins. After all, they lost a great deal of potential wealth as a direct result of the rezoning. Which raises the constitutional question: Did the city's new zoning rules amount to a taking under the law? And if it was a taking, what compensation was the city required to pay them? The Agins took their case to the Supreme Court, but the court's decision disappointed them. It ruled unanimously that the Tiburon zoning restriction did not amount to a taking. Moreover, the court believed that the Agins family was compensated by the general benefits brought about by the zoning change itself, which improved the environmental quality of life for all who lived in the area, including Dr. and Mrs. Agins.

To get a sense of the implications of the *Agins* ruling, consider how *The Washington Post* reported on the decision in 1980, under the headline "High Court Upholds Law Protecting Open Spaces." The first paragraph tells readers that the ruling showed that "zoning and land use laws that protect open space do not violate the rights of property owners."

The article goes on to say that, before the decision was final, environmentalists had a specific fear about the outcome: If the court *had* found that the sharp decrease in the Agins property brought on by the new zoning regulations *did* amount to a taking, and *did*, therefore, require just compensation not limited to the in-kind type, then similar regulations nationwide would grow massively more expensive to enact.[17] Thus, the court's ruling enabled a great deal of environmental zoning and regulation that might have been prevented by a decision more favorable to owners' property rights.

---

[17] David S. Broder, "High Court Upholds Law Protecting Open Spaces," *The Washington Post*, June 10, 1980, https://www.washingtonpost.com/archive/politics/1980/06/11/high-court-upholds-law-protecting-open-spaces/0198b371-4821-4f41-874c-a1947a4ebb1d/.

Environmentalists were jubilant. To Epstein, however, the court's ruling violated both the letter and spirit of the Constitution. It defined "taking" too narrowly, for starters, by failing to address the very real loss in property value suffered by the Agins. And by placing on the other side of the balance sheet the presumed environmental gain for the area, the decision failed again: The Agins' loss was vastly disproportionate to the benefit they shared with others, and thus nowhere near just compensation. In effect, their property was looted for the sake of others.

Takings and Taxes

Are taxes a form of takings? After all, a tax surely takes property, in the form of money, from private hands and transfers it to the public, presumably for the benefit of all. And taxes are, surely to some degree, coercive. In discussing taxes and takings, Epstein begins by acknowledging that taxes have been understood as legally different from takings, and he accepts the distinction. However, he raises another question about the differences between the two that is full of implications for the government's power of taxation. The question is not *whether* taxation differs from takings, but *how*. And, following close on the heels, whether taxation should follow the same rules that takings should.[18] For example, should taxes be used to fund only government projects that benefit the public generally?[19]

---

[18] Epstein, *Takings*, 283–284.

[19] We might also ask, uncomfortably, whether the public is compensated in a just way for what is taken through taxation by the spotty achievements of our governments.

Taken seriously, this line of questioning portends dire consequences for contemporary governance. Consider, for example, the various transfer payments made by government, which, as Epstein points out, make up a very sizable part of what our national government does now. These transfer payments occur in any program in which taxes paid to the government are paid back out to citizens on an unequal basis. If taxation must generally obey the rules of takings, the compensation derived from government programs must be just for the taxpayer. And this can hardly be done when the benefits go disproportionately to others. As Epstein writes, "As a matter of first principle, most of these [transfer] programs suffer fatal constitutional infirmities."[20]

To him, the takings clause sets a standard to which taxation should be held, if our Constitution is understood as a coherent, logical whole. In taxation as well as takings, our laws should protect private property by exacting a full cost from the state when its actions diminish that property; which is to say a just return to all taxpayers in terms of the benefits government provides. Over the decades, this protection has been degraded, enabling a vastly more active government than previously and more activist, in Epstein's assessment, than a proper understanding of the Constitution would allow.

Another Piece of the Puzzle: Contracts

We have seen how the takings clause might have provided a barrier against governmental activism but came to be understood in such a way that the barrier was dramatically lowered. Developments in another constitutional area, contracts, reveal a similar history.

---

[20] Epstein, *Takings*, 306.

Some background will clarify the importance of the issues at stake, and contracts, indeed, loom large in Epstein's understanding of our constitutional system. A contract is a legal agreement between parties that sets the terms for given interactions. An employee signs a contract with his or her employer, for example, that spells out what work is expected and for what pay. Or, a homeowner signs a contract with a builder to add a room to their house, also specifying expectations and pay.

The key feature of a contract, in Epstein's eyes, is that it is by design a win-win agreement. The two sides come together freely and settle on terms that each expects to be beneficial. And Epstein believes that contracts work; they are generally beneficial. The people entering into them know their own needs and have a strong incentive to sign only contracts that serve their interests.[21]

Moreover, contracts reflect the basic fact that we can accomplish more through cooperating with others than we can alone. To thrive, a shoemaker needs a steady supply of leather at a reasonable price. Likewise, a tanner needs a customer to buy his products. A contract brings the two together on terms each finds advantageous. While some competition between the signees is common and each will bargain to get the best possible deal from the other, their interests coincide and thus a mutually beneficial deal can be reached: Contracts grow out of natural reciprocity. The exchange at the heart of a contract "does not merely transfer physical or intangible assets. It increases human satisfaction by matching assets with the persons who value them most. . . . *Both* sides are better off than they were before."[22]

---

[21] See, for example, Epstein, *Simple Rules*, 72 and 78.

[22] Epstein, *Simple Rules*, 76.

Contracts also form a zone of free, private, sovereign action, which is, to some degree, inviolable against outside forces, including governmental action. As legal philosopher Lon Fuller put it, "A contract between two parties, in proper form and for a legitimate object, constitutes, as it were, a miniature statute."[23] The founders took this zone of protection seriously. Article I, Section 10 of the Constitution prevents states from passing laws that intrude into contracts and for a long time Supreme Court justices interpreted contractual obligations very strictly. Legal historian Lawrence Friedman called the contract one of the "sovereign notions" of the American republic during its first century and more.[24]

To give a sense of how seriously those obligations were taken in that earlier America, Epstein provides an example. It concerns a recurring legal dispute that arose between farmers and their hired help, where it was common for farmers to contract with a laborer for a year's worth of work in return for room, board, and a modest salary. However, laborers sometimes decided to leave ahead of time, breaking the contract. In such situations, what are the farmer's obligations to the hired helper? Some laborers who left early sued to get payment for the time they did serve, having partially fulfilled their obligations. But given that they failed to meet the terms of the contract, must the farmer pay?

When such suits came before them, judges typically sided with the farmer. In their eyes, the laborers made a promise when they agreed to the contract, and, in failing to live up to its terms, freed the farmer from any reciprocal obligation. For either party to back

---

[23] Lon Fuller, *The Anatomy of Law* (Praeger, 1968), 113.

[24] Lawrence M. Friedman, *A History of American Law* (Simon and Schuster, 1973), 464.

out of the contract's terms injures the other party. Farmers, for example, made plans based on the contracted labor. To meet those terms only partially is to simply fail and leave the farmer without the help he or she counted on. As one nineteenth-century judge in such a dispute, Levi Lincoln, wrote "in no case" has a contract been judged "to give a right to demand the agreed compensation, before the performance of the labor," and "the employer and the employed alike universally so understand it."[25]

In Judge Lincoln's words, Epstein sees something important about attitudes toward contracts in the nineteenth century. One is that the judge was clearly confident that his ruling was consistent with the prevailing customs, that people generally understand the obligations of contracts in this way. Also noteworthy is that the decision assumed an equality between the farmer and the laborer. The understanding was that both parties were competent to enter into the contract, able to meet its terms, and equally responsible for doing so. As Judge Lincoln also wrote in his opinion: "Nothing can be more unreasonable than that a man, who deliberately and wantonly violates an engagement, should be permitted to seek in a court of justice an indemnity from the consequences of his voluntary act. . . ."[26]

This sense of the sanctity of the contract is consistent with classical liberalism. Equality before the law is built in, government's role is largely confined to enforcement, and the power for making economic decisions is widely dispersed in private hands. By the same token, the responsibilities related to contracts were also widely dispersed. The nation, as classical liberals see things, reaped great

---

[25] For quotation, see Epstein, *Principles for a Free Society*, 162.

[26] Epstein, *Principles*, 163.

benefits from this economic regime, which, judging from results, encouraged strong growth and economic opportunity.

A great deal has changed since Judge Lincoln handed down his decision. While plenty of people today might still applaud the judge and the clarion terms in which he upheld contractual obligations, the place of contracts in our economic system is not what it once was. Among other things, the contract's zone of protection against outside interference has eroded dramatically.

The shift began in earnest during the late nineteenth and early twentieth centuries, as industrialization was remaking the nation's economic landscape. Among the prominent features of the day was the growing size and wealth of corporations. For some observers, the disparity in power between an employer—often a large company—and the employee called into question the whole idea of a legitimate contract between the two. Thus, the influential sociologist Lester Ward, wrote on this disparity: "Much of the discussion of 'equal rights' is utterly hollow. All the ado made over the system of contracts is surcharged with fallacy."[27]

For Ward and others, the changes brought by industrialization were drastic enough that the older notions that underpinned contracts were no longer sustainable. The deep imbalance between workers and their often powerful employers made new laws necessary, ones that would strengthen the laborer's position. Such arguments gave force to minimum wage and maximum hour laws passed in reaction to industrialization, both of which place constraints on contracts between employer and employee. If a law sets

---

[27] From Roscoe Pound's (once) well-known essay "Liberty of Contract," *Yale Law Journal* 18 (1909): 454.

a limit to the number of hours an employee works per week, he or she cannot opt for a contract that allows for more hours.

But maximum hour and minimum wage laws were only part of the story of increased government intervention in contracts. The notion that labor needed protection against the power of business was also behind the federal government's support for unions, which was made clear with the passage of the National Labor Relations Act of 1935. The National Labor Relations Act (NLRA) guaranteed employees in most sectors of the economy the right to unionize and engage in collective bargaining. By backing collective bargaining, the government dramatically altered the contractual landscape, forcing businesses to deal with workers en masse, and thus empowered, rather than as individuals. As Epstein puts it, the empowering of the labor unions, and especially the imposition of collective bargaining, "utterly displaces individual contracts between management and workers."[28]

This shift in government position was no minor matter. At its heart was the belief that the arrival of great corporations had driven the country past the era of individualism. Epstein quotes Justice Felix Frankfurter to this effect: "We are confronted by mass production and mass producers; the individual, in his industrial relations, but a cog in the great collectivity."[29] If men and women had become, in actuality, mere cogs in the big machinery of modern life, the nation's laws ought to reflect that, as the NLRA did.

---

[28] Epstein, *Principles*, 175.

[29] Richard A. Epstein, "The Monopolistic Vices of Progressive Constitutionalism," *Supreme Court Review* (2005), https://www.cato.org/sites/cato.org/files/serials/files/supreme-court-review/2005/9/progressiveconstitutionalism.pdf.

Frankfurter also wrote, rather alarmingly, that collective bargaining was "the starting point of the solution and not the solution itself." The older constitutional order diffused agency and responsibility widely; in the new era, this must give way to more centralized and, presumably, rationalized modes of decision-making. For, as Frankfurter continued, "it is through the collectivity, through enlisting its will and its wisdom, that the necessary increase in production alone will come."[30] Big business and big labor were two of the collective agents whose will and wisdom should determine economic direction. Another was big government itself.

Frankfurter's vision is close to a classical liberal's nightmare. Even though this version of the progressive future has not (exactly) come to pass, Epstein sees the passage of the NLRA as a regrettable step toward it.

Civil Rights in the Workplace

In time, another major entry point for government regulation of economic affairs would open and it would involve the rise of civil rights. The big changes in question are rooted in the Civil Rights Act of 1964, especially Title VII of the act, which "prohibits employment discrimination based on race, color, religion, sex, national origin, disability, or age."[31]

Crucially, this legislation established an office, the Equal Employment Opportunity Commission (EEOC), to enforce

---

[30] Richard Epstein, *How Progressives Rewrote the Constitution* (Cato Institute, 2006), 94.

[31] Federal Trade Commission, "Protections Against Discrimination and Other Prohibited Practices," https://www.ftc.gov/policy-notices/no-fear-act/protections-against-discrimination.

antidiscrimination laws in the workplace. The regulations in question cover hiring, firing, job advancement, workplace conditions and more. If a worker feels that they have been discriminated against on the basis of race, religion or any of the other categories, they can appeal to the EEOC for help. So, for example, if a female employee believes she has been denied a promotion due to her sex, she can ask the EEOC to investigate. And if the EEOC finds in her favor, the offending company will suffer the consequences.

Thus, civil rights legislation opens the way for government action in areas that had once been private, at least in the sense that they were not areas where government had authority to determine outcomes. The protections offered by Title VII do not extend to every business in the nation, but they do to most companies with fifteen or more employees and the bulk of the nation's work force is covered by its provisions. This means that most of the nation's employers have to take into account the oversight provided by the EEOC. Are enough women being hired and are they being hired for the right positions? Are people of color being promoted on par with similarly qualified white workers? Are the disabled treated fairly when it comes to hiring and promotion? The promise held out by Title VII is that government protections will put an end to workplace discrimination and allow the socioeconomic rise of people who had previously been left out.

In pursuit of this goal, the EEOC is highly active. In 2023, it investigated more than 80,000 total claims of discrimination with hundreds of thousands more investigations over the years.[32]

---

[32] U.S. Equal Employment Opportunity Commission, "Enforcement and Litigation Statistics," 2024, https://www.eeoc.gov/data/enforcement-and-litigation-statistics-0.

Employers cannot ignore this level of scrutiny, so it is certain that even firms that are not directly involved in EEOC actions will have taken measures to avoid discrimination-related trouble. Thus, Title VII and other civil rights laws have had an enormous impact on American business.

As a matter of principle, Title VII and its rules run counter to Epstein's understanding of how the Constitution should be interpreted. A government hewing to classical liberal ideals has no warrant to intrude in such a pervasive way into the economic lives of ordinary people. Employers and employees alike ought to be free to contract as they please, and government ought not to use its enormous power to tip the scale toward any group.

Apart from constitutional principle, however, Epstein also insists that the economic costs of antidiscrimination measures must also be taken into account. Through the oversight of the EEOC, we inject rigid, non-economic reasoning into arenas where economically productive decision-making is of the essence. Instead, the entry of civil rights concerns has, Epstein writes, "stifled innovation" by reducing the opportunities of employees "who did not meet some preconceived government conception of fair labor markets."[33] To the classical liberal, managers in business already have strong economic incentives to hire and promote workers based on merit, goals that would be undermined if they allowed prejudices to distort their views. That is to say, they have incentives to hire minorities, women, or disabled individuals so long as those people can contribute to a company.

---

[33] Epstein, *The Classical Liberal Constitution*, 180.

Imposing extraneous criteria on these decisions—race, sex, age, etc.—will likely lead to poor economic outcomes. And when those outcomes manifest themselves, correction can be difficult, given EEOC oversight. Addressing these matters, Epstein writes: "It is commonly said that no antidiscrimination law prevents an employer from firing a worker for incompetence. Literally understood, that claim is true, but in practice it is manifestly false given the risk of erroneous rulings [by government agencies]."[34] With the reach of antidiscrimination laws, Epstein believes that a great deal of economic inefficiency has been built into the system and we are paying the price. Epstein asks: "Now what is gained, if anything, by the use of so formidable a legal structure to attack the problem of discrimination? The answer is nothing, except social unrest and economic dislocation."[35]

Finally, because so many workplaces and so many employees are covered by EEOC regulations, there is another problem that Epstein insists we take into account. That is the cost of administering such a vast effort. Given the scope of its efforts, with the EEOC responding to employee complaints, documenting compliance by employers, and, where necessary, prosecuting legal cases, such administration can never be cheap.[36]

Partial Exceptions to Classical Liberalism

For Epstein, one of the attractions of classical liberalism is simply its effectiveness. If government policy follows its principles, he

---

[34] Epstein, *Simple Rules*, 174.

[35] Epstein, *Simple Rules*, 175.

[36] Epstein gives an in-depth analysis of administrative costs in *Simple Rules*, 30–36.

believes, the result will be a freer, more prosperous society. But there is a difference between being principled and being doctrinaire, and some social challenges test the practicability of the classical liberal approach. Here are two cases where Epstein sees some need to go beyond it to address major social or economic challenges.

The Challenge of Racism

One is anti-Black racism. In terms of employment, the presumption of classical liberalism is that management should be allowed to hire and fire as they see fit, without interference from the state, and their main concern should be job performance.

While this basic approach should guide our policies, Richard Epstein makes a qualified exception when it comes to race. The reason for this partial variance is the history of discrimination against African Americans, which was itself so thoroughly illiberal and destructive. With legalized segregation, violations against voting rights, and other discriminatory practices, the United States had "monopolistic structures put into place by government, supported by every conceivable device imaginable. . ."[37] to freeze African Americans out of the social contract. Because of this wholesale deprivation of civil rights—economic, political, and social—it was only reasonable, in Epstein's eyes, to accept the necessity of anti-discriminatory actions, including legislation such as the Civil Rights Act of 1964.

---

[37] Richard Epstein, "The Unfulfilled Promise of Anti-Discrimination Laws," *James Madison Program of American Ideals and Institutions*, video presentation, November 26, 2018, YouTube, https://www.youtube.com/watch?v=m1nIPDb57LE.

Acknowledging the need to "combat the vicious combination of public and private forces that created segregated institutions backed by the barrel of a gun,"[38] Epstein has embraced not only the goals of the Civil Rights Act of 1964, but also efforts to go beyond the color-blind language of the act (which, again, made it impermissible to discriminate against *any individual* on the basis of race, including, as logic would have it, white people).

He notes that in the aftermath of the act, and finding its immediate benefits insufficient, much of the nation's leadership understood the need to act more decisively than color-blind law would allow. In line with that strong current of feeling, the Supreme Court supported racially based affirmative action, for example. This more activist approach was "an accurate reflection of broad-scale political sentiment," as Epstein wrote, which demanded action in some practical form. "The forces for diversity and affirmative action are simply too strong to be denied,"[39] as he put it in 1995.

And yet, the very strength of this conviction, shared by so much of America's leadership, suggested to Epstein that the full power of the state need not be brought to bear on the private sector. "If the matter of discrimination were left to the market, the same political forces arrayed on behalf of affirmative action could still find their voice inside private organizations."[40]

Given a need to act, which Epstein accepts, the question arises: What is the appropriate role of government in pushing for civil rights improvement and how should it be balanced with private

---

[38] Epstein, *The Classical Liberal Constitution*, 536.

[39] Epstein, *Simple Rules*, 179–180.

[40] Epstein, *Simple Rules*, 180.

sector efforts? Epstein points to a Supreme Court case, *United Steelworkers of America v. Weber,* for some clarification. The case concerned an employee, Brian Weber, who worked for a company that had a training program, half of whose trainees were mandated to be African American. Weber, who was White, was passed over for the program and filed suit for discrimination. In their decision, the Supreme Court found the affirmative action program to be legal, with Weber losing his case. Ironically, one of the hurdles the court needed to clear was the insistence from Weber's side that color-blindness was written into the Civil Rights Act itself, and thus the favoring of African Americans in the training program was illegal.

So here was a case where an affirmative action effort, put into effect in the private sector, passed judicial review. Epstein notes a key effect of the ruling, that it opened the door to many more affirmative action programs in other companies, proving the willingness of private firms to act against discrimination.[41] Given the destructive legacy of institutional racism in this country as well as the desirability of better economic outcomes for African Americans, a classical liberal can see this as a positive development. This is especially the case where private firms were taking the lead. Leaving anti-discrimination programs in their hands meant that decisions could be made with a sensitivity to workplace realities that are unrealistic to expect when rigid legal decrees are handed down by the federal government.

For Epstein, something of the same logic was in play when Asian American students filed suit against Harvard University after they

[41] Richard A. Epstein, "How Affirmative Action Falls Short," *Defining Ideas,* Hoover Institution, October 6, 2020.

were rejected for admission to the school. While Epstein is critical of
Harvard for the specifics of its race-conscious admittance program,
he did not support the suit. "As a matter of first principle, I think that
Harvard University . . . should have the absolute right to determine
the students whom they admit and the grounds on which they admit
them."[42] Moreover, he points out that the job of selecting a body of
students is difficult, and that simply accepting them on the basis of
SAT scores, GPA, and similar standards might not yield optimal
results.[43] Why not leave this complicated task to the admissions staff-
ers who are immersed in its complexities and who can do their work
with some sensitivity to the nuances involved, rather than impose
decisions through legal fiat?

The Challenge of Common Resources

There is another area of law that tests the limits of classical liberalism, and especially its principled defense of property rights. It happens when the nature of a given resource, such as water or air, fits
poorly with the scheme of private ownership, and where its value
is most fully realized by treating it instead as part of the "social
commons."[44] And here, as Richard Epstein puts it, "too much of a
good thing can often prove to be a bad thing."[45] Generally, classical

---

[42] Richard A. Epstein "Harvard's Asian Exclusion," *Defining Ideas*, Hoover
Institution. August 6, 2018.

[43] These are lessons one can take from his discussion "The Unfulfilled Promise
of the Anti-Discrimination Laws," presented at Princeton University, Nov. 26,
2018. See especially his reflections on his own experience doing administrative
work at the university level and his conversations with Antonin Scalia on these
points. https://www.youtube.com/watch?v=m1nIPDb57LE.

[44] Epstein, *Principles for a Free Society*, 257.

[45] Epstein, *Principles for a Free Society*, 251.

liberals see private property as conducive to general prosperity, very much including the cases where owners' rights exclude others from its use. With resources in the social commons, however, that exclusivity is unworkable. As one example, Epstein points to seaways used for shipping by different nations.[46] Any attempt by one nation to claim exclusive rights over a seaway must lead to conflict, since other nations will want to use it as well. A situation where the oceans are treated as a commons to be shared by all is clearly the safer and more productive option.

With the example of the seaways in mind, Epstein notes that people have in fact found their way to informal, mutually beneficial practices for sharing shipping lanes on the sea: "[I]t is possible to develop—as were, in fact, developed—rules of the road that allow ships to pass each other in peace and safety even as they ply common waters on separate missions."[47] The incentive to find positive outcomes will often yield, over time, solutions beneficial for the parties involved.

At the same time, Epstein is under no illusion that the shared use of a common resource, such as the ocean, will prove easy in all cases. Negotiating the problem of ocean pollution comes to mind here, or the overfishing of the seas. Interested parties may try to take advantage of others and overuse or misuse the resource, especially if they see no credible threat of punishment. Some public enforcement might be necessary to maintain the common benefits of such resources—a matter made difficult in international cases where there is no overarching sovereign power to handle the enforcement of rules.

---

[46] Epstein, *Principles for a Free Society*, 261–262.

[47] Epstein, *Principles for a Free Society*, 262.

In context of policing the commons, Epstein mentions the legal concept of *nuisance,* which has deep roots in the common law tradition. This concept offers protection for property owners against those who, through their actions, infringe on the enjoyment of that property by others. To take a nineteenth century example, a gold mining company in California was sued because its standard practices, which included blasting land along rivers, led to large amounts of sediment flowing downstream. This, in turn, harmed others by making navigation and ordinary private enjoyment of the river more difficult. In an important decision, *Woodruff v. North Bloomfield Gravel Mining Co.*, a federal court sided with those downstream and against the mining firm. One cannot use a common resource in ways that harm others who have an equal right to enjoy it. If we return to the example of different nations sharing an ocean, the same principle should hold. If one party pollutes the water, it harms others and they, too, will have a legitimate case to make against the offender, with, perhaps, other nations acting in concert to punish them.

For Epstein, the nuisance framework respects property rights as much as possible, while encouraging economic development and, at the same time, discouraging the destruction of a common resource. By doing so, it offers a reasonable approach to the inevitable conflicts over the use of common resources.

Classical Liberalism and Civic Virtue

For critics of classical liberalism, one of its glaring faults is the presumed absence of concern for the common good. How could it be otherwise with a philosophy so devoted to personal liberties and self-interest, and an innate resistance to collective action? On the surface at least, Epstein's views fit this stereotype. Where others take it for granted that government action in pursuit of big, collective goals is necessary for achieving the best social outcomes, Epstein sees something else: a threat to liberty and a source of dysfunction.

But if Epstein is wary of arguments based on the common good and that lead to collective action, it is not because he disdains the actual good things we hold in common. His view is not that the goals of "common good" approaches are bad in themselves. Nor is prosperity the only thing we should aspire to. "Music, art, literature, science and humanitarian endeavors speak eloquently against such a view,"[48] he writes.

However, suggesting that it is government's job to pursue civic virtue and the common good is another matter, and Epstein won't take that step. Indeed, he sees it not only as beyond the government's remit, but as counterproductive. Chasing civic virtue, he says, is akin to pursuing happiness in one's personal life: "To make it the direct end of human conduct is to guarantee that it will not be obtained."[49] Just as personal happiness is more a by-product of sustained, fruitful effort, so too a healthy civic life is encouraged by productive activity. General prosperity, nourished by economic liberty, free markets, and strong property rights, provides a strong defense against aggression, conflict, and civic disorder, while providing the resources to foster the social goods that everyone wants. Classical liberalism works toward civic virtue "not by trumpeting

---

[48] Epstein, *Takings*, 344.

[49] Epstein, *Takings*, 344.

its evident goodness, but by creating a sound institutional environment where it can flourish."[50]

As Epstein sees it, we have already gone a long way down the wrong path in search of the elusive common good. In case after case—police power, the power of eminent domain, and the sanctity of contracts—barriers to government action have fallen across the board and government penetration into what once had been the private domain has continuously increased. The result has been, in Epstein's eyes, an accumulation of economic inefficiencies that have left the country poorer than it might have been, with less growth and fewer opportunities. With less of each, it comes as no surprise that the hoped-for effects of governmental action, including better futures for the widest possible swath of Americans, have not materialized, at least not to the degree supporters of activist government would have imagined.

The Danger of Faction

However serious these missteps may be, there is a still more troubling problem that, Epstein believes, is the natural result of our ambitious governmental pursuit of the common good. By seeking to redress unequal economic opportunities and social outcomes, government has responded with policies that treat different classes of citizens unequally. These include progressive taxation and redistributive spending, as well as regulatory policies that "take" from some without just compensation. But allowing the unequal treatment of citizens

---

[50] Epstein, *Takings*, 345. But note that in context Epstein says specifically that eminent domain (properly understood) is what encourages civic virtue, not "classical liberalism," as I put it here. However, it seems clear from his writings that my extension to the more general term fits well with Epstein's thought.

sends a message to the public: The government will take sides on the various issues that roil society, including those touching on race, gender, class, and other identities. By taking sides, the government alters the relationship between citizen and government, and so, too, the relationships among citizens.

Those who are not direct beneficiaries of government action understand well enough that the government is not acting on their behalf and resent the fact. To others, the message is perhaps worse: not just that government might not help them, but that government is itself a promising route to pursue the things they want. Organized pressure groups might, for example, lobby for financial support, as do dairy farmers and many other groups. For others, the government, with its massive, coercive power, can serve ideological or partisan ends. Given the strength and reach of government, Epstein believes that we cannot simply assume that its agencies will act out of neutral, common good motives. It should come as no surprise that the Environmental Protection Agency, for example, might attract employees with strong environmental ethics who would see the agency as a vehicle to achieve their preferred ends. Similar dynamics draw people to other government bureaus and departments. As Epstein comments, federal agencies "take strong ideological positions on the issues that come before them time after time. . . . The ostensible expertise of agency personnel is little more than a pretext for a strong one-sided commitment which skews the distribution of power" within our governing system.[51]

The message that government's job is, in part, to redistribute wealth or other goods filters through the whole of our political

---

[51] Epstein, *Principles for a Free Society*, 237.

discourse. To the degree it is embraced, our politics become a battle for benefits in a zero-sum game, or even, as Epstein puts it, "a subdued version of the war of all against all."[52]

This competition for the favor of the state is especially dangerous as we become, inevitably in such an environment, more and more factionalized. Once a policy issue is raised within government, coalitions will form to serve preferred agendas and given how many areas of our lives government touches, these blocs "can coalesce around any issue" and "organize along any natural fault lines: occupation, region, race, religion, or sex."[53]

To Epstein, this whole approach to governing is unsustainable and focuses our attention on the wrong place. Rather than expand the role of government in our lives, we should return our focus to more productive private activity. We should return, as it were, to the spirit of the contract: join with others to plan, build, create, and accomplish fruitful ends. A contract forms the basis for a mutually productive relationship, not one that simply transfers goods from one party to another. They increase society's overall wealth, rather than squander it in factionalized brawling. They point toward the future instead of indulging either nostalgia for a supposedly more social past or illusions about hunting down an elusive "great society" in the future. This is the classical liberal view.

---

[52] Epstein, *Takings*, 344.

[53] Epstein, *The Classical Liberal Constitution*, 21.

Chapter 2

A PROGRESSIVE VIEW

Classical liberalism faced an existential crisis in the early twentieth century when the industrial era exploded in the United States. With the enormous changes brought by industrialization, urbanization, mass immigration, and technological breakthroughs, the United States had to decide whether to navigate the new world with its older, more laissez-faire constitutionalism in place, or rewire its laws to meet the new challenges. In the end, and through a process that unfolded over decades, the nation chose the latter course. For Richard Epstein, this was exactly the wrong choice, as he made clear in his 1995 book, *Simple Rules for a Complex World*. In his view, we attempted to manage our destiny through "a massive increase in the frequency and complexity of the legal rules that govern society." That approach, however, had matters backward. "The proper response to more complex societies should be ever greater reliance on simple legal rules, including older rules too often and too easily dismissed as curious relics of some bygone horse-and-buggy age."[1]

The Pressure to Change

Having followed the other path as a nation, we should better understand how and why we departed from the classical liberal way. And we should question whether Epstein was wrong and we actually needed deep constitutional change to survive the transition to a modern economy.

Consider the impact of the changes that the nation confronted. We mentioned some in the previous chapter, but development brought challenges that reached nearly every aspect of life. Among the results of heavy industrialization, for example, were more dangerous workplaces and industrial-scale pollution. The effects extended beyond the immediate consequences of industrialization to, for instance, education, where it was believed that a modern economy required a workforce prepared to meet its specific demands. To Epstein, such challenges would have been met with better results under the old constitutional rules. But under the pressure of events, American government initiated any number of projects and programs to address challenges that arose with economic development, and such interventions became the norm.

It should be noted that popular support ushered in these big constitutional changes, which arrived on a swell of legislative will. That is, the will of lawmakers and other elected officials to pass legislation intended to address given problems. To Richard Epstein, the courts should have kept the lawmakers within traditional

---

[1] Epstein, *Simple Rules*, 21.

constitutional channels. However, after offering temporary resistance, the courts failed to do so. Additionally, since the New Deal especially, the political acceptability of more active government has remained fairly solid. If the American people have qualms about Social Security, workplace safety regulations, massive infrastructure projects, and related governmental efforts, those qualms have not been potent enough to overturn these long-standing features of American governance.

Progressivism: Some Basics

For the purposes of this book, we describe the twentieth-century departure from classical liberalism generally as *progressive,* using the term in a particular way. In the sense meant here, progressivism is, naturally, a movement that embraces change. Progressives are those among us who are quickest to see our failings and most ready to address them. Progressives believe in progress.

But progressivism entails more than just an awareness of problems and a *desire* to fix them. Progressives also tend toward a confidence that we *can* solve problems. They are, relatively speaking, less concerned than classical liberals or conservatives about the inevitable costs of government action; nor are they as concerned about unexpected and unwanted consequences of action. With that self-assurance, progressives are willing to take on big problems, such as those that arose with industrialism. In addition, they understand that solving such problems requires commensurate force, which generally means enhanced governmental power, and this does not worry them unduly. Thus, the progressive project has depended on stretching traditional understandings of the Constitution in order to find that power.

A classic example can be seen in the much-noted *Lochner* deci-sion of 1905 and its overturning about thirty years later. The *Loch-ner* case relates to a law passed by the New York state legislature in 1895, which limited the number of hours employees in bakeries could work. According to the law, those employees could work no more than ten hours per day or sixty hours per week. The justifica-tion was health. Bakery jobs were physically demanding and over-work in them could cause personal harm, so the argument went. Joseph Lochner, a bakery owner, was charged with violating this law because some of his employees exceeded the legally prescribed limits. Lochner fought the indictment, claiming that he and his employees had a right to determine the number of hours worked and that the law trespassed on this right.

In a 1905 decision, the Supreme Court sided with Lochner. The right of employers and employees to agree to their preferred terms, including the number of hours worked, was protected by the Four-teenth Amendment, according to which "no State can deprive any person of life, liberty, or property without due process of law." Infringement on the terms employees and workers agreed to (their "liberty of contract") was an unconstitutional imposition on the right to freely use one's own labor, a form of property as Locke taught.

Under pressure, however, the Court evolved. Change came with a 1937 Supreme Court case, *West Coast Hotel Co. v. Parrish,* which concerned a Washington law that set a statewide minimum wage for women. The Court's decision here is generally thought to have ended the "Lochner Era." Writing for the court, Chief Justice Charles Evans Hughes noted that the Constitution does not mention the liberty of contract anywhere. Moreover, liberty more generally requires "laws against the evils that menace the health, safety, morals and welfare of the people."[2] This is the police power, now understood to allow the state into relations between employer and employee in ways previously thought off limits. Thus, if the legislative will can be found to pass such laws, the Court would no longer block them.

It is worth looking at the political pressures that contributed to the Court's change of heart on the matter. The *West Coast Hotel* decision came in the midst of the Great Depression and just after Franklin D. Roosevelt's smashing victory in his reelection bid of 1936. Before that victory, the Supreme Court had blocked a good deal of Roosevelt's more ambitious domestic policies. After it, the judiciary substantially gave up its opposition.[3] For both classical liberals and progressives, this shift was a watershed in America's constitutional history.

The Administrative State

Along with the newfound powers provided by the "living" Constitution, there is another pillar of progressive governance worth mentioning here. It is the *administrative state*. This "state" comprises any number of agencies, largely but not exclusively in the executive branch, which exist to administer government policies. Theoretically at least, laws are passed by legislatures and these agencies simply put them into effect. Since the beginning of the Progressive Era, more ambitious government has meant more work for the administrative state, which has grown enormously over the decades.

---

[2] *West Coast Hotel v. Parrish*, 300 U.S. 379 (1937).

[3] Another key to the Supreme Court's turnaround is that Roosevelt was able to nominate his own choices for open positions on the court, which, after the president's long tenure in the office came to reflect his views more and more.

Looking back to the early twentieth century, one can get a sense of how progressivism and the administrative bureaucracy have been joined at the hip from the start. Consider the Forest Service, an agency within the Department of Agriculture, which was founded in 1905. It provides a classic example of a progressive agency at work (and, perhaps, at its best). For starters, the Forest Service was established to address problems that arose with the industrial era. Specifically, by the early twentieth century, new technologies and systems of organization were turning logging companies into a formidable force for leveling trees. Their efficiency was a boon for business and for consumers—the companies produced lots of inexpensive wood for building—but by 1905 it was growing clear that, without change, their aggressive cutting was putting terrible stress on the forests themselves. In addition to the potential loss of timber, there was growing evidence that deforestation was linked to other problems, including soil erosion and flooding.

The growing awareness of these dangers came in part from the academy. The first American graduate program in forestry, at the Yale Forest School, was founded in 1900. As Americans groped for solutions to deforestation, they drew on the improving science of forestry, as developed at Yale and other universities.

A partial, practical solution to the problem came with the founding of the Forest Service, which could apply the latest research to preserving the health of the national forests.[4] The goal was to improve management practices on these lands and make them more

---

[4] The national forests are federal property, amounting to over 188 million acres of land today. The first "Forest Reserve" was established in 1891; the name "National Forest" was used for these lands starting in 1907, according to the Forest History Society; see https://foresthistory.org.

productive and sustainable resources for the future. To accomplish this, they needed to answer various technical questions: How much cutting can a forest sustain, given differing climates, terrains, and soil types? How should replanting be handled and with what tree stock, given, again, the diversity of the nation's land?

Crucially, and bearing on important constitutional questions, such specialized knowledge cannot be expected from any legislature. The legislators themselves will not have the necessary training, nor can laws easily be written with enough specificity to address all the variations in the nation's forests. What legislatures can do, however, is pass laws that set up agencies such as the Forest Service and delegate power to them for developing policies to meet the demand for better forestry practices. However, doing so entails an important shift of power from the elected members of the legislative branch to the unelected staff found in an executive agency, such as the Forest Service.

We see a pattern here that has been repeated many times elsewhere in government. To meet developing challenges, agencies are established where expertise can be concentrated; the agency then becomes a de facto policymaker in given areas: the Department of Transportation, NASA, the Environmental Protection Agency, the Occupational Safety and Health Administration and so forth, each in its particular arena. One can also see how the development of the administrative state fits with the progressive ethos: Problems are identified; agencies, staffed with experts, are founded; and such agencies are granted powers to address those problems.

On the constitutional path we have followed for the last hundred and twenty years, an increased reliance on the administrative state has been a central feature.

Cass Sunstein

By the understanding of *progressive* outlined above, Cass Sunstein is very much a progressive, and an important one as well. Immensely prolific, he has written dozens of books and hundreds of articles, and has, in addition, worked in the federal government as head of the Office of Information and Regulatory Affairs under President Barack Obama. He also served as a constitutional consultant to the post-apartheid government of South Africa, as well as consulting with other foreign governments.[5] As of 2025, Sunstein teaches law at Harvard University, having previously taught at the University of Chicago for over twenty years. He is one of the most cited legal scholars in the United States.[6]

Sunstein's views stand in stark contrast to those of Richard Epstein and the differences are deeply rooted. They include contrasting views on that central constitutional issue, property rights. Recall that Epstein embraces Locke's views on property, which serve as a foundation for much of his constitutional thought. As a reminder, according to Locke, property is generated through personal effort and individuals legitimately claim exclusive rights over property when they take possession of resources from their natural state. One of government's fundamental jobs is to protect property against aggression from others.

Sunstein will have little of this. In his view, the social contract theory is a story with no basis in reality, and there is no categorical right to property. What we have instead are laws, written by

---

[5] "Sunstein, Cass R. 1954-," *Encyclopedia.com*, https://www.encyclopedia.com/arts/educational-magazines/sunstein-cass-r-1954.

[6] See the Series Editor's Foreword to Sunstein's 2021 book *Liars: Falsehoods and Free Speech in an Age of Deception* (Oxford University Press, 2021), xi.

mortals, that establish and protect property rights. "[P]roperty rights do not come from the sky or even from nature. Property rights as we understand them have legal sources."[7]

Sunstein held similarly deflating views about two related doctrines favored by Epstein and other classical liberals. He described laissez-faire as a "myth," adding that it is "a grotesque misdescription [*sic*] of what free markets actually require and entail."[8] And markets themselves, which we might take to have a reality independent of politics and prior to government, are also human artifacts: "[M]arkets are legally constructed instruments, created by human beings hoping to produce a successful system of social ordering." Sunstein has also written that "[M]arkets are a particular form of government intervention."[9]

Certain conclusions follow from these assertions. Most obviously, if property rights and markets are *not* prior to our laws but created by them, there is no need to act as if they are sacrosanct. Instead, we can change our laws as they relate to property and markets if we expect those changes to improve society. This logic is essential to progressive doctrine and Sunstein certainly adheres to it. So, for instance, the *Lochner* decision (defending the "liberty of contracts") was, in his words, "infamous and discredited"[10] and there is no constitutional barrier to economic interventions such as maximum hour and minimum wage laws.

---

[7] Cass Sunstein, *Legal Reasoning and Political Conflict* (Oxford University Press, 1996), 85.

[8] Cass Sunstein, *Free Markets and Social Justice* (Oxford University Press, 1997), 5.

[9] Sunstein, *Free Markets*, 384.

[10] Sunstein, *Free Markets*, 229.

Nor, for that matter, is there any legitimate constitutional barrier to the rest of the New Deal program. Once again, the jurisprudence that supported the New Deal should not be underestimated as a dramatic change of constitutional course. To Sunstein, it "represented a fundamental restructuring of the American legal system,"[11] one in which the "original understanding of a sharply constrained central government was . . . repudiated by the nation."[12]

As an example, consider the New Deal agricultural program. The Great Depression hit farmers hard, and among their problems was a decline in commodity prices: many farmers could not get good prices for the crops they raised, leaving them unable to make a decent living. To meet this and other challenges in the agricultural sector, President Roosevelt proposed and Congress passed the Agricultural Adjustment Act (AAA) of 1938.[13] Among the resulting programs was one in which economists within the Department of Agriculture set limits on how much farmers could raise of certain crops. Cuts in production would lead, so the thinking went, to a beneficial rise in commodity prices. Setting those production quotas was a matter for economists in the Department of Agriculture to decide, rather than for markets to sort out.

The Commerce Clause

The degree of activism here, with a governmental department setting quotas for farm crops, reflects a serious departure from

---

[11] Sunstein, *Free Markets*, 319.

[12] Sunstein, *Free Markets*, 350–351.

[13] Roosevelt had previously passed an even more ambitious AAA in 1933, but the Supreme Court had struck down key provisions of that legislation in 1936. The AAA of 1938 was a revised effort to achieve similar ends.

previous assumptions about the regulatory powers of the federal government. At the heart of the Supreme Court's change of direction was a reinterpretation of the Constitution's Commerce Clause. The clause appears in Article 1, Section 8 where the specific powers of Congress are enumerated. Among them, Congress has the power to "regulate Commerce with foreign Nations, among the several States, and with the Indian Tribes." The traditional understanding of these words, as they relate to domestic matters, was that Congress could step in to smooth out barriers that made trade across state lines difficult. Under this old understanding, Congress was enabled by the Commerce Clause to establish a nationwide zone of relatively free trade.[14]

At the time of the New Deal, however, sharp legal minds took a fresh look at the Commerce Clause and decided that it held previously unsuspected depths. In time, the Supreme Court came to understand the Commerce Clause as empowering the national government to pass laws not just to encourage interstate trade, but to regulate it in surprisingly intrusive ways. Consider, for example, a 1942 decision, *Wickard v. Filburn.* Roscoe Filburn was an Ohio farmer charged with violating limits set on the crops he raised, having planted twelve more acres of wheat than the quota allowed. He defended himself, however, by pointing out that he used the extra wheat for feeding his livestock and for making flour for his family. Since the wheat in question was not sold, it was not part of any commerce, let alone interstate commerce.

[14] See National Constitution Center, "The Commerce Clause," https://constitutioncenter.org/interactive-constitution/interpretation/article-i/clauses/752 for background.

The Supreme Court disagreed. Though the amount of wheat in question was small and though he used it on his own farm, what Filburn produced had an effect on the wheat market as a whole.[15] If this seems to stretch the Commerce Clause powers beyond recognition, so be it. As the Court said in another decision (*United States v. Darby*), the "power of Congress over interstate commerce is *not confined to the regulation of commerce* among the states."[16]

The New Deal vs. the Chicago Way

From a constitutional perspective, progressives, including Cass Sunstein, find the New Deal perfectly legitimate. Since property rights, liberty of contract, and free markets are not inviolable, indeed are creations of the state, the state has every right to reengineer them. In the case of the New Deal, incursions into these areas should be seen as a constitutional, and reasonable, response to challenges posed by difficult historical circumstances.

However, accepting the legitimacy of the New Deal-era regulations is not the same as accepting their efficacy, a point Sunstein acknowledges. Part of what makes his thought interesting, and perhaps an indicator of where of our constitutional future lies, is the way it has evolved beyond progressive positions of earlier periods. In fact, without wishing its reforms away, Sunstein has been sharply critical of the New Deal and its approaches to policy, and he has proposed a notably different path toward progressive reform.

---

[15] *Wickard v. Filburn,* 317 U.S. 111 (1942), https://supreme.justia.com/cases/federal/us/317/111/.

[16] *United States v. Darby,* 312 U.S. 100 (1941), https://supreme.justia.com/cases/federal/us/312/100/.

The new directions Sunstein embraces surely reflect his experiences at the University of Chicago, where he joined the law faculty in 1981. Recalling his years there, he wrote that "giants roamed the Earth and called Hyde Park their home."[17] The giants he referred to were his fellow faculty members at Chicago's law school, and, critically, of the university's economics department as well. They included three Nobel Prize winners—George Stigler, Ronald Coase, and Gary Becker, all in economics—as well as such highly influential legal scholars Richard Posner and Frank Easterbrook (both of whom became federal judges). This stellar faculty also included Richard Epstein, whom we've met. The interdisciplinary aspect was crucial, with professors of law drawing deeply on what the economists were learning and teaching.

These were unsentimental thinkers, "quick, funny, witty, cutting, tough, confident, and occasionally brutal," as Sunstein remembers them.[18] An important aspect of their economic work was to scrutinize human behavior and analyze the findings to see as clearly as possible how people actually behave when faced with economic choices. Among the lessons learned, to take Gary Becker's work as an important example, is that people generally act in ways that maximize outcomes for themselves.[19] If this sounds banal, it is not when applied to policy. For example, policy makers cannot expect people to react to regulation as if self-interest suddenly did not

---

[17] Cass Sunstein, *Simpler: The Future of Government* (Simon and Schuster, 2013), 51.

[18] Sunstein, *Simpler*, 51.

[19] For a very brief overview, see David R. Henderson, "Gary Stanley Becker, 1930-2014," *Econlib*, The Library of Economics and Liberty, https://www.econlib.org/library/Enc/bios/Becker.html.

apply. Take the case of rent control. When rents seem unaffordable in a given city, progressives have often called for limits on what landlords can charge. This might work in a static system, but real life is far from that. Rather than simply accepting the new price regime, landlords, acting in self-interest, might respond by switching their rental units to other purposes, for example. This has the unwanted effect of reducing the supply of units available and putting upward pressure on housing costs, a self-defeating—or iatrogenic—outcome for rent-controllers.

That the economic system is dynamic and not readily subject to simple controls is unwelcome news to progressives, who depend on predictable outcomes from their interventions. But the dynamism is real and regulators must take that into account. This is something the University of Chicago faculty understood in spades, and their economic judgments often skewed against state controls. "What I have always found to be the Chicago view," said Becker, "is that free markets do a good job. They are not perfect, but governments do a worse job."[20]

Sunstein could not have helped being influenced by the extraordinary minds at Chicago and the intellectual climate there. He could not help, for example, to recognize the importance of property rights, including their political value. In his 1997 book *Free Markets and Social Justice,* Sunstein writes that the "right to own private property has an important and salutary effect on the citizens' relationship with the state . . . and can be seen as a

[20] John Cassidy, "Interview with Gary Becker," *The New Yorker,* January 14, 2010, https://www.newyorker.com/news/john-cassidy/interview-with-gary-becker.

necessary precondition for the status of citizenship."[21] In a similar vein, he wrote about the virtues of free markets, saying that "in some situations, constitutions themselves should protect free markets," and that "market-oriented policies are far better in the areas of health, safety, and the environment than is generally recognized."[22]

Neither comment means that Sunstein sets property rights or free markets on sacred ground where they are immune to legislative adjustment—far from it. But he understands the power of both and could hardly have thought otherwise given his years at the University of Chicago.

Next Generation Progressivism

Consistent with the lessons in the air at Chicago, Sunstein came to view the New Deal with critical distance. In hindsight, its approach to economic regulation appeared too top-down, too directive, too punitive, and too insulated from actual results. In Sunstein's eyes, the legacy of this approach was a regulatory system that was, among other things, "extraordinarily inefficient."[23]

His answer to this problem was not, as free market purists might have preferred, to cast off the regulatory project entirely. Rather, it would be to turn the power of economic and scientific analysis toward improving the effort. A crucial step in this direction, one that Sunstein has supported, was to impose cost-benefit analysis on government programs.

---

[21] Cass R. Sunstein, *Free Markets and Social Justice* (Oxford University Press, 1997), 208.

[22] Sunstein, *Free Markets*, 7.

[23] Sunstein, *Free Markets*, 322.

The essence of cost-benefit analysis is so straightforward and commonsensical that one might assume it had always been in place. Before imposing a new policy, government agencies should weigh its presumed benefits against the costs of implementing it. But cost-benefit analysis, as it is put into effect by government, implies a more thorough scrutiny, with the analysis better grounded in economic theory and available data than previously attempted.

Consider how cost-benefit analysis might affect environmental regulations. Everyone wants cleaner, healthier air to breathe, but are the benefits of a given regulation worth the expense? Did it make sense, for example, to ban lead from gasoline, as we did in the not-too-distant past?[24] The ban brought substantial costs—automakers had to adapt their engines to lead-free gas and retool their plants to build the new motors. And petrochemical companies had to retool to produce the new lead-free fuels. None of this was free and the costs to the industries involved would have negative consequences for the broader economy, such as more expensive cars. Cost-benefit analysis requires that such costs be quantified before imposing the ban.

In addition, the analysis calls for regulators to assess the benefits of removing lead from gas. We know that lead is dangerous to our health, but cost-benefit analysis demands that we quantify this as well. Does lead in the environment actually lead to negative health consequences? What exactly are those consequences? How significantly would removing lead from gasoline decrease the ill

---

[24] The phase-out came slowly, beginning in the 1970s, with the use of leaded gas for on-road vehicles ending as of 1996; see https://www.eia.gov/energyexplained/gasoline/history-of-gasoline.php#:~:text=Leaded%20gasoline%20was%20eventually%20taken,as%20of%20January%201%2C%201996.

effects? Finally, do the expected benefits from de-leading outweigh the costs involved?

It sounds grim to weigh the inestimable value of good health in economic terms, but cost-benefit analysis calls for just that. So government regulators must sometimes speak in terms of the mortality risks associated with, for instance, toxins released into our environment though industry or agriculture. The use of one pesticide might be expected to cause one hundred deaths per million persons, and if so it should perhaps be banned. Another toxin might be expected to cause ten deaths per hundred million persons and its ban might not survive cost-benefit analysis. Of course, such deliberations raise a painful question: How much is a life worth? There is actually a term that applies here, the Value of a Statistical Life, or VSL. And different governmental agencies use slightly different formulas to set theirs. For the Department of Transportation, to take just one example, the VSL was $13.2 million as of 2023.[25]

In 1981, Ronald Reagan issued an executive order to make cost-benefit analysis standard practice across executive branch agencies.[26] Since that time, the practice has brought about something of a revolution in the nation's regulatory regime, one that, in Sunstein's eyes, makes federal regulations more efficient and

---

[25] U.S. Department of Transportation, "Departmental Guidance on Valuation of a Statistical Life in Economic Analysis, May 7, 2024. https://www.transportation.gov/office-policy/transportation-policy/revised-departmental-guidance-on-valuation-of-a-statistical-life-in-economic-analysis.

[26] "Presidential Executive Order 12291 (Ronald Reagan, 1981), *Ballotpedia*; https://ballotpedia.org/Presidential_Executive_Order_12291_ (Ronald_Reagan,_1981)

evenhanded.[27] It is also a system that was born from, and in practice depends on, an understanding of economics that has improved a great deal since the heyday of the New Deal. In drawing on academic scholarship, cost-benefit analysis is very much in the lineage of American progressivism, however distant it seems from the bighearted, openhanded liberalism we might associate with, say, Tip O'Neill or, for that matter, from the public rhetoric that actually inspires contemporary progressives.

More Social Science

Having embraced cost-benefit analysis, Sunstein has also looked to social sciences for other tools to improve regulatory policy. His interest in behavioral science[28] has led him, for example, to see *nudges* as a useful way for the government to address some of the problems Americans face. Behaviorism is the school of psychology that examines how behavior is conditioned by external stimuli. For regulators, nudges are the stimuli, designed to bring about preferred responses. They can take various forms, but as an example, think of the way the federal government has discouraged tobacco use. When government requires that cigarette packages include a warning about the dangers of smoking, this is a nudge. The warning is

---

[27] "Even in theory, CBA can help discipline and systematize important aspects of the policy-making process. . . . policymakers should view CBA as a tool to inform thoughtful decision making, not as some uniquely scientific method of analysis that dictates what must be done." Sunstein, *Free Markets and Social Justice*, 138.

[28] According to his Harvard faculty page, Sunstein is the founder and director of the Program on Behavior Economics and Public Policy at Harvard as well as a participant in the WHO's advisory group on Behavioural Insights and Sciences for Health, and an adviser to the Behavioural Insights Team in the United Kingdom. See https://hls.harvard.edu/faculty/cass-r-sunstein/.

aimed to influence citizens as they make choices. At the same time, the warning leaves the final decision of whether to smoke or not in citizens' hands, and in this sense is not directly restrictive. A nudge differs from an outright regulation, as Sunstein says, in that it aims to "influence decisions while preserving freedom of choice."[29] Of course the government also taxes cigarettes, which can be seen as more coercive and thus taxes are not really nudges, lying somewhere between a nudge and an outright ban.

Tobacco warning labels are familiar by now, having been issued for decades. Since they first appeared, behavioral psychologists have been at work, refining their understanding of how people absorb information and how they respond to it. As they proceed, regulators look for ways to make use of these advances. In his book *Simpler,* Sunstein discusses various ways that psychology can be applied to policy, including a form of nudging called *choice architecture.* This is a technique for framing options when we are in a position to make a choice, but doing so in a way that encourages a particular outcome. To illustrate, Sunstein describes shopping at an IKEA store. He describes these stores as "hopelessly confusing." But the confusion, Sunstein believes, is by design. Wandering down their aisles in a state of frustration, seeing all sorts of goods they hadn't previously wanted, potential buyers are inclined to purchase items on impulse.[30] Whether or not this is IKEA's formal strategy, one can be certain that they, and other retailers, spend a good deal of effort on planning store layout in order to put customers in a frame of mind to spend money.

---

[29] Sunstein, *Simpler,* 38.

[30] Sunstein, *Simpler,* 60.

Sunstein believes that government can use similar techniques to nudge American citizens toward better, healthier choices in their lives. By carefully structuring the information we encounter, policy makers can shape the outcome of our choices. As a successful example, Sunstein draws on his own experience in government during the Obama administration. At that time, the Department of Agriculture was updating the food pyramid label once seen on packaging, which was used to promote healthy eating. As it existed for many years, the pyramid was so dense with confusing information that one could hardly make out any clear message about what to eat. To remedy this, communications experts collaborated with nutritionists to come up with a new visual. The result was a graphic food plate, which, according to Sunstein, presented a much clearer dietary message. The choice architecture was improved and as a result citizens are nudged toward a healthier diet.[31]

Government uses many similar nudges of the sort we have all seen: mileage stickers on cars we might buy, or the "energy-guide" stickers on refrigerators and clothes dryers that allow consumers to easily compare the efficiency of competing models. Nudging can take other forms, however, including some that assume a less active, more passive role for citizens and thus perhaps less freedom in the choice architecture. Consider, for example, the use of default settings in interactions citizens make when dealing with the government. Default settings are familiar, and they can be hugely helpful. If you buy a computer in the United States, take it home, and start to use it, you will find certain applications loaded up already—by default—and when you open them, English will be the language

---

[31] Sunstein, *Simpler*, 75–77.

used on them—default again. By making certain aspects of our life automatic, default settings can make life a great deal easier.

Government agencies can use defaults not just for simplifying given tasks, but for improving the health of citizens. What if, for example, the federal government automatically enrolled people in an organ donation program as a default position? There could be an easy way to opt out, preserving the freedom to take part or not. But by making organ donation the default, government could immediately increase the number of organs available for emergency transplants, with substantial benefits for seriously ill people. In Austria, where, as Sunstein pointed out in 2013, the default favors organ donation, the rate of consent was over 99 percent; in Germany, by contrast, which does not assume consent, the rate was around 12 percent.[32] To Sunstein, the lesson is clear. By reframing the choice on organ transplanting, government can dramatically improve public health.

We must add, however, that such reframing will not be limited to any narrow range of issues. Among its virtues, a nudge is cheap to implement and seems not to violate constitutional boundaries. So why limit their application to just a few situations? Sunstein understands that governmental nudges are often seen as manipulative and insidious, and even agrees that they are clearly paternalistic.[33] However, government will find it hard to turn away from such techniques, when they promise solid returns on low-cost investments. As Sunstein describes them, nudges involve a "small shift in

[32] Sunstein, *Simpler*, 103.
[33] Sunstein, *Simpler*, 190–191.

the social environment that can make a big difference."[34] Unless we have a constitutional change of course, look for more, and more sophisticated, nudges in our future governance.

Worst-Case Scenarios

The question of what tools government should have at its disposal grows more urgent when the nation confronts potentially disastrous threats. Looming over our public discourse in recent years are dangers that would test the limits of governmental capabilities should they come to pass. Cass Sunstein explores the question of how government should respond to such profound challenges— including potential damages from climate change and terrorist attacks—in his 2007 book *Worst-Case Scenarios*. In it, Sunstein applies lessons he has absorbed throughout his career, both as a legal expert and as a student of human behavior.

The result is not pessimism about meeting such challenges, but a call to realism in facing them. Sunstein is wary, with such high stakes, of two dangers, both of which are natural pitfalls as behavioral science indicates. One is the temptation to ignore threats in their more catastrophic forms. Ignoring dangers might actually be useful as a self-defense mechanism. We face potential threats every time we leave home, and perhaps a deep instinct for survival turns our attention away from them and toward less paralyzing lines of thought. Still, it is better to be aware of threats and take preventative actions when possible.

At the same time, we are also prone to the opposite danger, focusing on worst-case scenarios in a way that leads to self-defeating

---

[34] Sunstein, *Simpler*, 39.

outcomes. For example, in the wake of the September 11 attacks of 2001, many people were gripped by fear of terrorist strikes involving airplanes. That fear led some people to switch from flying to driving long distances. Since driving is more dangerous than flying, though, this led to an uptick in travel-related deaths, an increase that likely numbered in the thousands.[35]

So, as Sunstein sees things, the first step in formulating sound policy for worst-case scenarios is to assess risks and benefits accurately, both those associated with the threat itself and those associated with potential solutions. But we can see how complicated these assessments can be if we look at the case of climate change. While many scientists seem certain about general trends related to the climate, there is much less certainty about detailed predictions of future catastrophes. Thus, as Sunstein writes, "nations may be operating in the domain of uncertainty . . . in the sense that they are able to identify the worst outcomes without being able to specify the likelihood that they will occur."[36]

So it seems that the best we can manage is to estimate a range of possible climate outcomes with differing likelihoods. Perhaps a catastrophic threat, such as dramatically rising seas combined with severe global drought, is possible but unlikely within a given timeframe; meanwhile, a less devastating result, such as a modest sea-level rise, is more likely over that period.

For Sunstein, it is critical to develop the most detailed analysis possible about potential developments and impacts. How many lives will be lost in given scenarios? How much economic damage

[35] Cass Sunstein, *Worst-Case Scenarios* (Cambridge: Harvard University Press, 2007), 139.

[36] Sunstein, *Worst-Case Scenarios*, 26.

done? How should we account for negative effects that are not easily quantifiable, such as the potential loss of animal species or ecosystems? The calculus is made far more complicated when we add the costs of preventive actions. If we take the most extreme protective measures to head off the worst-case scenarios, they could impose serious economic damages. And those costs will not be limited to property; economic deprivation will cost lives, too, perhaps especially in developing countries.

The complexity of formulating climate-related policy should already be obvious, but from there the complexities continue to mount. Sunstein notes that time is another complicating factor. If rising carbon dioxide in the atmosphere is driving climate change, it makes sense to start cutting carbon emissions as soon as possible. However, Sunstein cautions against acting too quickly. Taking drastic action in the short run brings its own risks. If those actions cause heavy economic damages, the losses could make us more prone to disaster in the long run. A poorer society, for example, will be generally less able to develop technologies that could reduce future emissions effectively. Back in 2007, Sunstein wrote: "Perhaps climate change will produce less serious harm than we expect, because adaptation will be possible, or technology will be able to reduce warming." If the effectiveness of our actions depends on an accurate assessment of risks, that assessment must take into account the likelihood of advances in technology.[37]

Who Should Act?

Given the compounding complexities involved in addressing climate change, a constitutional question arises. Any profound understanding

---

[37] Sunstein, *Worst-Case Scenarios*, 256–257.

of climate science is well beyond the grasp of nearly everyone and missteps could result in serious social and environmental damage. So who in the American system should have authority to make climate policy?

Over time, Sunstein has been consistent in his confidence in expert opinion and the capabilities of our regulatory agencies. By contrast, his faith in Congress has been limited. In commenting on the legislature's capacities, Sunstein has described Congress as "a group of generalist representatives—all with many issues to address, few with particular expertise in regulatory law, and many beholden to special interests," adding that the legislature should restrict itself to "generalities."[38] Thus, the regulatory agencies, with deeper expertise in the relevant law and in the science, would seem far better suited to producing the regulations that apply to climate concerns.

This, however, raises still more difficulties. According to the original constitutional vision, Congress is the primary institution for setting the basic direction for the nation's domestic (especially) policy. Congress can, and does, delegate a great deal of authority to the regulatory agencies, but Congress, representing the people, has a heavy responsibility for establishing the national government's goals. What if it cannot bring itself to do so with climate issues? And as of early 2025, it has not, at least not in any definitive fashion.

Yet even if one acknowledges the strengths of the regulatory agencies in relation to the legislature, one understands that they must have the sanction of Congressional support in our constitutional system. The agencies need leeway to do their work effectively,

---

[38] Sunstein, *Free Markets*, 349.

but too much looseness in the connection to legislation would deprive regulators of their democratic legitimacy.

The tension here, where the progressive will to act meets a constitution that makes action difficult, should be familiar. It is, effectively, the same problem Woodrow Wilson faced in his time. Now the stakes are even higher, if the worst prospects of the climate change scenario are assumed. Back in the first half of the twentieth century, the Constitution, or at least the dominant interpretation of it, was forced to evolve. Today one wonders: Will the pressure of climate-related threats—which are existential according to activists—force constitutional change to deal with them?

And what if it doesn't? One crucial difference between then and now: In the past, popular support swung behind progressive change, especially during the presidency of Franklin D. Roosevelt. So far nothing like that has happened, despite constant media attention to climate-related issues for many years now. Without that popular support, any constitutional change that would allow dramatic action on the challenge would be revolutionary indeed.

Democracy, Deliberation, and Free Speech

Professor Sunstein's interest in regulatory policy has been near the heart of his legal thought. But to focus exclusively on that aspect of his career risks doing him an injustice, since his constitutional scholarship has another major area of focus. This aspect is more social and cultural, and includes knotty problems related to what might be called democratic rights. And this subject is not only of great interest to Sunstein, it has been central to the progressive movement in recent decades as well.

Democracy is a complex term, with various facets. In exploring democracy and its related rights, Sunstein restates, and to some degree accepts, the classical liberal approach to cultural issues. According to it, our democratic constitutional order accepts people as they are, in all their diversity, and does not concern itself with changing them. Instead, government is, in Sunstein's words, "above all respectful of the diverse conceptions of the good held by its many constituents." Democracy allows for the free play of interests on the part of all citizens and understands that self-interest is "the usual motivating force of political behavior." Government's job is to accept these impulses and sift them in search of majorities that will yield policy on an ad hoc basis, rather than on any preordained order.[39] That is the classical liberal view.

But for Sunstein, while there is much to accept here, it is not enough. The classical liberal take on the Constitution fails to do justice to another aspect of the founders' system, one that Sunstein identifies especially with James Madison's thought. This aspect emphasizes the *deliberative* element in democracy. There is in the very nature of deliberation a creative potential that our Constitution was designed to foster. Rather than accepting a static confrontation of self-interested views, deliberation leads naturally to the transformation of views, which Sunstein embraces and emphasizes in his constitutionalism.

One touchstone for his views is Madison's *Federalist* no. 10. There, Madison addresses the distinction between democratic and republican forms of government, which in turn bears directly on the concept of deliberation. The key lies in the nature of representation.

---

[39] Sunstein, *Free Markets*, 13.

Where democracy directly translates the wishes of the people into policy, Madison's view of republicanism encourages something more indirect, subtle, and positive. According to Madison, the people elect representatives who, he hoped, would possess unusual wisdom and thoughtfulness. When these representatives go to Congress, they do not simply vote "yea" or "nay" according to the wishes of their constituents. Instead, they deliberate among them-selves in a discourse with the power to "refine and enlarge" the views of those involved, as Madison put it. The resulting decisions, transformed from the raw wishes of the people, provide the legiti-mate basis for our governance. Sunstein takes this line of thought a good deal further, saying, "we might even define political truth as the outcome of [the] deliberative process. . . ."[40]

In making this claim, Sunstein places extraordinary faith in the potential of deliberation to improve society, as Madison himself perhaps did. But Sunstein's views on deliberative democracy extend beyond those of Madison in important ways. Where Madison saw Congress as the crucial focal point for that deliberation and empha-sized the elite standing and capabilities of its members, Sunstein takes a broader view. For starters, his extensive writings on free speech make clear that he views our democratic deliberation as reaching far beyond legislatures, encompassing a broad range of conversations across various media.

Sunstein also emphasizes that this discourse must be genuinely democratic. For this deliberation to achieve its fullest promise, Sun-stein says it must meet certain conditions, one of which is a standard of "political equality," as he puts it, "in which arguments matter but

---

[40] Cass Sunstein, *Democracy and the Problem of Free Speech* (The Free Press, 1993), 19.

power and authority do not." For discourse to be equal, it must be inclusive. "A well-functioning democracy requires a degree of citizen participation . . . and large disparities in political (as opposed to economic) equality are damaging to democratic aspirations."[41]

Given this, one might assume that Sunstein would be happy with our current information free-for-all, where media of all sorts teem with opinions of every variety. What he advocates, however, is not that, and here there is a parallel with his attitude toward *laissez-faire* in economics. Just as a free market in economics is not some pure, natural ideal, so it is with the market in ideas. Left simply to unregulated forces, our public discourse will fall short of what the country needs to move forward. Sunstein cites some specific concerns with the pure market model: It might lead to an informational world with "little or no high-quality fare for children," one that encourages "widespread political apathy or ignorance," and that allows "social balkanization in which most people's consumption choices simply reinforce their own prejudices and platitudes, or worse."[42]

The threat of insularity is of special concern to Sunstein. "It is easily imaginable that well-functioning markets in communications will bring about a situation in which many of those interested in politics merely fortify their own unreflective judgments and are exposed to little or nothing in the way of competing views," unchallenged by a media that too often presents "a bland, watered-down version of conventional morality. . . ."[43]

---

[41] Sunstein, *Free Markets*, 171.

[42] Sunstein, *Free Markets*, 171.

[43] Sunstein, *Free Markets*, 171–172.

Social Norms

Here, Sunstein's dismissive mention of "conventional morality" is worth noting, important as it is to understanding his views on deliberation, democracy, and progress. What it points to is his often adversarial opinion in relation to social norms and customs. In his 1997 book *Free Markets and Social Justice*, he devotes a chapter to social norms, in which he asserts, as Richard Epstein does, their importance. "I urge that behavior is pervasively a function of social norms; that changes in norms might be the best way to improve individual and social well-being. . . ."[44] The importance of social norms clearly applies to matters of racial and sexual equality, matters that Sunstein, a strong supporter of civil rights, has written about extensively. Not surprisingly, he finds a laissez-faire attitude toward social norms to be akin to free markets in other regards: It implies a neutral starting point that does not actually exist, while benefiting some at the expense of others; and, in any case a free market in norms is insufficient to ensure social progress. Government, Sunstein believes, "deserves to have, and in any case inevitably does have, a large role in 'norm management.'"[45]

A central deficiency of the free market in norms is that we carry into our social relations preconceived notions that are often discriminatory. In Sunstein's eyes, such prejudicial attitudes can become so deeply embedded as to seem "natural," as he puts it.[46] Consider how women have been viewed historically. While men and women do differ in certain respects, some differences are due

---

[44] Sunstein, *Free Markets*, 34.

[45] Sunstein, *Free Markets*, 34.

[46] Sunstein, *Free Markets*, 43.

to the imposition of preconceived notions, being "an outcome of inequality or its product." He adds:

> Differences in physical strength, for example, would certainly exist without inequality, but such differences as there are now undoubtedly have a good deal to do with expectations, nutrition, and training. These differences cannot solely be attributed to women's sexual and reproductive capacities. Indeed, the degree of difference between men and women is notoriously variable across time and space. These variations are sufficient to show that what society attributes to nature is often a social product.

To break the grip of preconceived notions, our political discourse cannot rest content with the mere repetition of conventional opinions, and a "free" market in ideas will not provide the necessary correctives.

Speech Markets

In other words, government action might be necessary to make sure that social norms will be contested. To bring this about, Sunstein has explicitly called for a New Deal for free speech, which would provide a reset for our public discourse, just as Roosevelt's New Deal did for economic rights. This New Deal for speech would include regulatory efforts to "ensure diversity of view and attention to public affairs" and to "promote both political deliberation and political democracy."[47]

---

[47] Sunstein, *Democracy*, xix.

As with his views on economic matters, Sunstein does not see the free informational market as bad in itself and indeed sees it as having strengths that ought to be preserved. Free markets in speech, he wrote in 1993, are "content-neutral, at least on their face," which is important because "no government official is authorized to decide who will be allowed to speak."[48] Commenting on the dramatic expansion of free speech rights in the second half of the twentieth century, he writes that this "revolution accomplished enormous good," and it is "fully appropriate to celebrate our tradition of liberty and to recognize that ours is an extraordinary and precious achievement."[49] Still, the dangers of relying solely on market forces make it necessary to improve on what we have.

In keeping with the lesson that regulations work best when they are not simple, top-down commands, Sunstein suggests less-directive fixes. Government could, for example, provide guidelines to broadcasters for improving coverage of public affairs, ones that encourage the presentation of diverse views; government could also provide subsidies for the same; and it could use its regulatory power to grant free media time to candidates during election seasons. In certain cases—college campuses, for example—Sunstein has been open to implementing speech codes that ban hateful rhetoric, so long as they are ideologically neutral.[50] These are nudges, as it were, that he believes can foster a better discourse, which in turn will make for a better future.

---

[48] Sunstein, *Democracy*, 119.

[49] Sunstein, *Democracy*, 250.

[50] Sunstein, *Democracy*, 203.

And, once again, public discourse is fundamental to Sunstein's understanding of the American political system: "Much of the American Constitution can be understood as an effort to set out the preconditions for political deliberation; the First Amendment is only the most conspicuous example."[51]

Free Speech and Misinformation

Professor Sunstein believes that public deliberation, crucial as it is, faces a serious challenge today in the form of misinformation. His concern led him to write the book *Liars: Falsehoods and Free Speech in an Age of Deception,* published in 2021. In it, he explores the confusing landscape where citizens are inundated by vast amounts of information, with some being good but far too much being bad. Faced with this, Sunstein seeks a way to purge at least some of the bad information while retaining a basic freedom of speech.

In the book's opening chapter, he makes clear that his preference is for open discourse, which allows for the airing of even deceptive and dishonest speech: "In general, falsehoods ought not to be censored or regulated, even if they are lies."[52] And he makes that statement knowing that lies can lead to real trouble. Sunstein wrote *Liars* in the early months of the COVID-19 pandemic and he claims that bad information at the time, which led people to take the virus less seriously than they might have, was likely responsible

---

[51] Sunstein, *Democracy,* 247.

[52] Cass Sunstein, *Liars: Falsehoods and Free Speech in an Age of Deception* (Oxford University Press, 2021), 3.

for unnecessary levels of illness and death.[53] Still, he remains wary of the government acting as censor, not least because that power would threaten oppositional viewpoints. "If officials are licensed to punish falsehoods, they will end up punishing dissent."[54]

Yet open discourse, so necessary to good civic health, need not put falsehoods on the same plane as truths, and government has long held various tools for combating misinformation. If dishonest speech involves libel, for example, it is punishable under the law; laws against perjury have also provided society with a defense against public lies; and there are laws against fraudulent advertising: Cigarette makers, for example, cannot claim their products are beneficial to users' health. All these measures restrict speech in one way or another and are entirely legal.

Looking closely at such laws and drawing on major Supreme Court decisions related to free speech,[55] Sunstein sees four factors that undergird government's rightful limitations on speech. These factors are:

1. The speaker's state of mind: Did they know they were wrong, for example, or were they simply mistaken?

2. The magnitude of harm caused: Were many people adversely affected by given wrongful claims, or few, or none at all?

---

[53] In this regard, see Sunstein's discussion of a Leonardo Bursztyn study contrasting the health effects of Tucker Carlson's COVID-related discussions with those of Sean Hannity's; Sunstein, *Liars*, 109–110.

[54] Sunstein, *Liars*, 3.

[55] These include *Schenk v. The United States*, *New York Times v. Sullivan*, *The United States v. Alvarez*, and others.

3. The likelihood of harm: Was harm a predictable effect of speech or unlikely?

4. Timing: One act of speech might lead to immediate ill effects, such as crying "Fire!" in a crowded theater, or the potential harm might be very distant, as in saying "The world will end in 2099!"[56] The former might be banned, the latter cannot.

Even if one favors free speech, Sunstein believes there are cases where these four factors allow for legitimate restrictions on speech, going beyond traditional libel or perjury. But he emphasizes that censorship and punishment are not the only tools government can use to counter misinformation, and that warning labels and similar nudges can be used effectively against misinformation without encroaching on core First Amendment rights.[57]

Yet government's responsibilities cover only part of the challenge of misinformation. Sunstein also looks at the role of private corporations, especially those in the social media world, in maintaining a healthy information system. Companies such as Facebook, Google, and Twitter/X have an enormous impact on what we all read and see. Moreover, the technologies they use to sift and present information are not only powerful, but potentially dangerous: "With algorithms and personalization, those who spread falsehoods are increasingly able to reach receptive audiences and tailor the messages to them. The problem is only going to get worse."[58]

---

[56] For Sunstein's framing of these four factors, see Sunstein, *Liars*, 128–129.

[57] Sunstein, *Liars*, 133.

[58] Sunstein, *Liars*, 124–125.

So company policies related to misinformation are crucial to public discourse.

Of course, private companies are not bound to the same constitutional standards that government is, so they have a different set of tools at their disposal for dealing with misinformation. Sunstein notes that major social media companies have taken their responsibilities in this area seriously, responding with sets of policies that ban some content. Facebook, for instance, will not publish certain *deepfake* videos, which can present lifelike representations of public figures doing or saying things they never imagined. Deepfakes can also be taken down for showing graphic violence or nudity.[59] Nor is Facebook alone; other companies have also put their own measures in place to remove harmful content and to label or otherwise curate controversial materials.[60]

Whether such controls are keeping pace with the mischief done by misinformation is another matter. Writing in his book *Liars*, Sunstein was clearly frustrated by the mainstreaming of views that, for example, questioned the dangers presented by COVID-19, as well as views skeptical of public health measures taken against the virus's spread. In his eyes, the problem of bad information is rampant and a matter of great concern. Sunstein states flatly: "Private institutions . . . should be acting more aggressively to control . . . falsehoods and lies. They should be doing more than they are now

[59] Sunstein, *Liars*, 120–121.

[60] NB: Many conservative or libertarian commentators have expressed frustration that internal efforts by such companies have reflected the biases of their corporate cultures. This controversy has continued for several years, especially in relation to Twitter/X under the leadership of Elon Musk, who has taken a stand against the perceived progressive censorship and in favor of freer speech on his platform.

doing to prevent the spread of misinformation involving health and safety and of doctored videos."[61]

Constitutions: Designing Democracy

It can hardly be overstated how important political discourse is to Sunstein's constitutional thought. He places deliberation at the heart of politics and has great faith in its potential for reshaping societies. That faith was put to a severe test when he was invited to consult with South African authorities as they wrote a new constitution for that country's post-apartheid era.[62] Apartheid was the society-wide order of racial segregation, dominated by a small white minority. It was formally established in 1948 but had deep legal and cultural precedents going back to South Africa's colonization by the Dutch in the seventeenth century.

Apartheid fell in the national elections of 1994, the anniversary of which is now celebrated in South Africa as Freedom Day. With this momentous shift, the need for a new constitution was clear, but so, too, were the immense challenges of re-forming the nation politically. Not only was it necessary to throw out its old constitution, but also to uproot much more than just the law. The whole society had been ordered around racial discrimination, so any new constitution would have to take that history into account and, obviously, chart a new course.

With regard to this difficult constitutional starting point, Sunstein refers to a distinction made by fellow legal scholar Lawrence

---

[61] Sunstein, *Liars*, 133.

[62] Sunstein reflected on this experience in his book *Designing Democracy: What Constitutions Do* (Oxford University Press, 2001).

Lessig between *preservative* and *transformative* constitutions. As
the terms suggest, preservative constitutions aim to conserve
long-standing practices and social arrangements. Transformative
ones, by contrast, "attempt not to preserve an idealized past, but
to point the way toward an ideal future."[63] In the case of South
Africa, the need for transformation was such that its new constitution explicitly opposed the nation's segregationist history. As the
nation's constitutional court has stated: "There is a stark and dramatic difference between the past in which South Africans were
trapped and the future on which the Constitution is premised."[64]

Against this background, where long-denied rights had to be
reestablished by a new constitution, and indeed a whole society
recast, Sunstein had to think deeply about the foundations on which
to ground basic rights. Among the possibilities were two that he
found insufficient. First is what he calls *metaphysical realism*, the
belief that "humans can have access to something wholly external
to human judgment and cognition,"[65] a reality that would provide
a sound basis for establishing the rights of all. For Sunstein, while
the underlying philosophical issues related to metaphysical realism
are difficult to sift, they are also moot. In *Designing Democracy*,
he writes: "[As] participants in a constitutional culture, few people
seriously believe that constitutional rights should be identified by
exploring a point of view that is external to human perceptions,
needs, and interests."[66]

---

[63] Sunstein, *Designing Democracy*, 68.

[64] Sunstein, *Designing Democracy*, 68.

[65] Sunstein, *Designing Democracy*, 73.

[66] Sunstein, *Designing Democracy*, 73.

If metaphysics won't provide the foundation for rights, Sunstein considers whether tradition can. That is, whether we inherit an understanding of rights from customs and practices that evolved historically, ones that we might accept as authoritative and a guide for the future. Here, again, Sunstein demurs. Leaving aside a clear case, such as South Africa's, where national traditions have been so deeply marked by racial discrimination, he still finds tradition deeply suspect as a foundation for rights. Among other problems, traditions are often complex and self-contradictory, as is seen in the case of the United States. Our traditions, Sunstein points out, "include race and sex discrimination as well as considerable censorship of dissent and disregard for the interests of the poor—alongside mounting freedom of speech and religion and an anticaste principle. . . ."[67] Rather than providing clear support for rights, traditions are often murky in this way, and as such an uncertain basis for protecting them.

Characteristically, Sunstein believes that we are not just called to look elsewhere for new foundations, but to stand in rational judgment on our traditions in order to move forward. This we can only do through self-criticism. When traditional practices are challenged on constitutional grounds, "we cannot know whether those practices are defensible until we have done some investigating."[68] This investigation comes about through deliberation, which must include the voices of the marginalized and their particular "perceptions, needs, and interests." What emerges from this deliberation will, Sunstein hopes, provide the best practical protection for our rights, and constitutions must encourage such debate and reflection,

---

[67] Sunstein, *Designing Democracy*, 82.

[68] Sunstein, *Designing Democracy*, 87.

however painful they might be. This holds for South Africa in its extreme case, and for the United States as well.

The principle here is central to Sunstein's constitutional thought. Under a properly functioning, democratic constitution, deliberation will not only drive policy, but will also be the ground of its legitimacy. Constitutions that do not encourage, or at least allow, self-critical discourse rightly lose the democratic basis they need. Sound constitutions, by contrast, ensure that policies are tested against a wide range of opinions, so that acts of government are "justified not by the fact that a majority is in favor, but on the basis of reasons that can be seen, by all or by almost all citizens, as public regarding."[69]

By holding government to this standard, a constitution will tend toward a certain dynamic. For starters, the ideal of deliberative democracy will militate "against second-class citizenship for anyone,"[70] since democracy itself implies inclusivity and seeks to draw marginalized groups into the mainstream of society. A built-in anticaste principle will also find economic and social deprivation unacceptable. In considering governmental measures to improve the lot of the marginalized, we might see the US Constitution as rule-bound in a way that makes it difficult to enact such policies. However, an emphasis on deliberative democracy, Sunstein believes, will tend to dissolve hard barriers against activist government, barriers that have defined traditional constitutionalism in many minds. "[B]y ensuring reason-giving, by increasing exposure of diverse views, and by prohibiting second-class citizenship,"

---

[69] Sunstein, *Designing Democracy*, 239.

[70] Sunstein, *Designing Democracy*, 242.

he says, "a democratic constitution goes a long way toward promoting a wide range of social goals, emphatically including justice itself."[71]

---

[71] Sunstein, *Designing Democracy*, 243.

Chapter 3

CLASSICAL CONSTITUTIONALISM

There is a remarkable overlap between Cass Sunstein's deeply progressive constitutional views and those of the far more conservative Adrian Vermeule. Indeed, the two co-wrote a book, *Law and Leviathan: Redeeming the Administrative State,* a full-throated defense of the federal government's powerful regulatory agencies. But the differences between the two are of greater importance. Where Sunstein looks for political truth in the transformative outcomes of democratic discourse, at least as he defines democratic, Vermeule looks elsewhere, as we will see.

Adrian Vermeule is the Ralph S. Tyler, Jr. Professor of Constitutional Law at Harvard Law School. Born in 1968, and thus a generation younger than either Sunstein or Richard Epstein, he is a similarly productive scholar, having written or co-written eight books plus dozens of articles and essays.

Vermeule's background is worth reviewing since it shaped his mature constitutional thought in important ways. He grew up in

Cambridge, Massachusetts where his mother, Emily, taught archae-
ology and classical philology at Harvard. His father was also a
scholar, curator of the classical art collection at the Museum of Fine
Arts in Boston. Thus, Vermeule was exposed to Greek and Roman
culture when young, spending vacation time in various locations
throughout the eastern Mediterranean, including Greece, Cyprus,
and Turkey.[1]

After his secondary education, Vermeule attended Harvard
himself. There he studied classical Chinese philosophy, learning
Mandarin, and graduated summa cum laude in 1990. The scope
of this education, encompassing both classical Western and Chinese
thought, has given him a perspective on American law that might
otherwise have been impossible. Vermeule has many critics, but
none can fault him for parochialism.[2]

When done with his undergraduate work, Vermeule studied at
the Harvard Law School, from which he graduated in 1993, again
summa cum laude. His timing was fortunate in certain respects.
By that time there was crucial institutional support in place for
brilliant young conservative legal scholars. This came in good
measure from the Federalist Society. Founded in the early 1980s by
law students at Harvard, Yale, and the University of Chicago, the
society grew out of the frustration of conservatives with the

---

[1] Brooke Masters, "Adrian Vermeule's Legal Theories Illuminate a Growing
Rift Among US Conservatives," *Financial Times*, Oct. 13, 2022.

[2] On Twitter/X, Jan. 24, 2024, he wrote: "A thought on legal theory, especially for younger academics and lawyers: there's a big, wide world out there
waiting to be explored. . . . Get outside the Anglosphere and learn new
stuff—talk to continental Europeans, Latin Americans, Asians, and others.
And absorb some legal theory from the Western and other traditions, from
before the mid-20th century narrowing of the Anglo-American legal mind."

dominance of progressivism in the legal academy. Once the first Federalist meeting was held, the movement spread quickly, with students and sympathetic faculty establishing chapters on many campuses over the next decade. Since then, the organization has had an impressive impact by nurturing conservative legal talent; as of 2025, five of the Supreme Court justices have been affiliated with it, including Brett Kavanaugh, Neil Gorsuch, Amy Coney Barrett, Clarence Thomas, and Samuel Alito.

Vermeule benefited from the Federalist Society network, which, among other things, brought promising young lawyers to the attention of judges looking for clerks.[3] Not long after graduating from law school, Vermeule was hired by judge David Sentelle on the D. C. Circuit Court of Appeals, and when done there moved on to clerk for Supreme Court Justice Antonin Scalia. He made a mark in these positions, with Sentelle describing Vermeule as the first person to serve both himself and Scalia and to be "a conservatizing influence" on each.[4]

Vermeule on Originalism and the Administrative State

If the Federalist Society provided institutional support for rising conservatives, originalism provided their legal doctrine. And just as the Federalist Society was a response to the institutional dominance of progressives, so originalism challenged the dominance of progressive legal theories in the courts. The Warren and Burger-led Supreme Court came in for particular criticism from originalists, who believed that constitutional interpretation had grown so loose

---

[3] Masters, "Adrian Vermeule's Legal Theories," 2022.

[4] Masters, "Adrian Vermeule's Legal Theories," 2022.

during those years as to be virtually unmoored from the essential purposes of the Constitution. This was especially true in relation to the "rights revolution" of the 1960s and '70s. Broadly speaking, the term refers to the dramatic expansion of individual rights, where the target might be either governmental abuse or putatively repressive social standards. In deciding various cases related to personal rights, Supreme Court decisions touched on any number of sensitive points in American life: the rights of the accused in the criminal justice system; the rights of religious (or anti-religious) dissenters in relation to school prayer; the rights of flag burners and others in free speech cases, and much more, including, of course, civil rights cases as they related to race and sex.

(Here, it is worth noting a basic fact concerning rights: They are always claims made by a given party against others, and when vindicated these claims always impose some obligation on others. For example, when individuals successfully claim a right to publish sexually explicit materials, the broader society is obligated to accept their publication.)

The case of abortion rights and *Roe v. Wade* illustrates the dynamic that originalists opposed. Prior to *Roe*, abortion was regulated at the state level guided by laws passed by state legislatures. The results varied, with some states effectively banning the practice and others allowing it on relatively liberal terms. With the *Roe* decision, the Supreme Court overrode this settlement and defined abortion as a constitutional right, at least to this degree: The practice was legally protected through the first trimester, though states held some authority to regulate it after that.

To the originalists, this was egregious overreaching by the Supreme Court and a violation of constitutional standards. In nationalizing abortion law, the *Roe* decision bypassed state legislatures, which, originalists argued, were the legitimate authorities for regulating the practice. The problem, as originalists framed the issue, was procedural as much as it was substantive. With *Roe*, the federal judiciary circumvented the proper procedure and thereby prevented the views of the people from being taken into account through the traditional constitutional means—legislation. In its place, the Supreme Court imposed its own views on the matter, which, given the makeup of the Court, naturally leaned progressive.

To restrain the judiciary and prevent it from imposing its will in this fashion, originalism proposed a basic rule for interpreting the law. Judges must make their decisions in accordance with the words and intentions of a law's authors, including the authors of our basic law, found in the Constitution. Disciplined by this rule, judges would be less able to make decisions according to their own values, as originalist critics believed was happening.

In the early years of its development, originalism was immensely appealing to conservatives and classical liberals. But for Vermeule its basic approach presented difficulties that were obscure at the start of the movement but fatal in the long run. And Vermeule's career has been, in many respects, about coming to grips with those shortcomings.

Vermeule on Checks and Balances

If originalists demand that judges be faithful to the terms and intentions of the founders, one constitutional doctrine that would seem inviolable is that of "checks and balances." Near the heart of the Constitution is the separation of government into the three familiar branches—legislative, executive, and judicial. As the standard understanding of the Constitution has it, the powers of each branch are defined in such a way that they limit each other, preventing a dangerous concentration of power in any. If originalists look for authority in the founding vision of the Constitution, they can hardly fail to embrace its system of checks and balances. And, in fact, one of the core complaints of the originalists was that the judiciary frequently overstepped its legal bounds and was "legislating from the bench," as in the case of *Roe*.

Vermeule, however, takes a decidedly non-originalist view of checks and balances. His interpretation of the matter can be found partly in his book *The Executive Unbound: After the Madisonian Republic*, co-written with Eric Posner. As the title suggests, the book examines the power of the executive branch, which, as the authors make clear, has come to dominate the other branches, legislative and judicial. With this development, the internal balances of the founders' Constitution have been dramatically altered.

To understand how this came about, one can return to the question of whether dramatic social and economic change made it inevitable that government would respond by intervening more in social and economic affairs. Vermeule and Posner accept that the answer is yes: Industrialization, urbanization, and radical, ongoing technological advances, taken together, present challenges that make more active government virtually inescapable. Libertarians might argue that we could have met these complex, rapidly evolving developments without expanding government intervention into previously private affairs. But even if possible in theory, political realities were such that we did not. The growth of government, for Vermeule and Posner, was all but inevitable.

If history leads to expansive government, it also leads to a stronger executive branch, with its many departments, bureaus, and agencies. Vermeule and Posner note, as did Cass Sunstein, that the burden of running regulatory agencies, and gathering the expertise needed to guide them, leads to a bigger role for the executive branch. This is reflected in the much greater size of today's executive, with two million civilian employees (not including another 1.4 million military service members) versus thirty thousand in the legislative.[5]

Vermeule and Posner add more, however. The executive branch is also much better suited to modern administration on organizational grounds than the legislative. By contrast, the legislative branch suffers from institutional debilities, one of which is its democratic structure. Built into the idea of a representative legislature is the equality of its members. This equality makes power more diffuse in Congress and weakens its ability to act decisively. Another debility of the legislative branch is the balky set of procedures that Congress (and other American legislatures) operate under, some stemming from its bicameral structure.[6] By design, the legislative process is sluggish and cumbersome.

This procedural balkiness makes Congress slow to act in the face of challenges. By contrast, the executive offices can be far more responsive to the challenges presented by ever-changing modern realities, at least as Vermeule and Posner see things. As a result, the executive has gained policymaking initiative in relation to the legislative, which has grown more reactive and become less of a policy

---

[5] Eric Posner and Adrian Vermeule, *The Executive Unbound* (Oxford University Press, 2010), 29. Note that the book was published in 2010 and specific figures have changed over time.

[6] Nebraska's state legislature is an exception, with a unicameral structure.

leader over the last century. But to the authors of *The Executive Unbound*, this is less a violation of our constitutional heritage than an organic development within it, even if that development has stretched traditional constitutional understandings.[7]

Or perhaps more than stretched them. To the founders, while the branches were intended to balance each other, Congress was something of a first among equals. Since the people themselves were sovereign, it was natural that their elected representatives would hold the power to determine national policy. So, when Vermeule and Posner point to the steady weakening of the legislative branch and the contrasting empowerment of the executive, they are calling attention to a major departure from the founders' constitutional vision. This, needless to say, is a long way from the originalism so many conservatives of Vermeule's generation were drawn to.

Vermeule on Administrative Law

Just as the executive branch has grown to overshadow the legislative, it has also come to overbalance the judicial branch. This is one lesson Adrian Vermeule learned from his close study of administrative law, the body of law that governs, among other things, the regulatory agencies and their powers. As we've seen, these agencies are charged with putting laws, passed by legislatures, into effect, and this means writing specific regulations to achieve legislative goals. Since those regulations must be applied to an ever-evolving landscape, the regulator's job involves creatively interpreting the legislature's wishes. Just how creatively and how freely the agencies can act is a key question addressed by administrative law.

---

[7] Posner and Vermeule, *The Executive Unbound*, 50–52 and 208–209.

The answer has been, in short, quite freely. And not only do the administrative agencies have a good deal of latitude in writing regulations, they have also gained the authority to judge when their regulations have been violated and even to punish the offenders. If, for example, your business is investigated by the Occupational Safety and Health Administration (OSHA), it will be OSHA that decides whether you are in violation of their regulations, and OSHA that will set your penalty. Moreover, if you want to appeal their decision, the appeal will likely go back to OSHA unless there is something unusual about the case. Likewise with other agencies, and thus the regulators effectively take on the three basic roles of governance: the legislative (in writing the regulations), the executive, and the judicial.

Professor Vermeule is an excellent guide to how this accumulation of power has come about, and two of his books are especially valuable for that. They are *Law's Abnegation: From Law's Empire to the Administrative State* and *Law and Leviathan: Redeeming the Administrative State,* which he co-authored with Cass Sunstein. In them, Vermeule not only examines how the regulatory agencies grew so powerful but also defends that development.

First, consider the judiciary's presumed role in relation to the regulators, that of oversight. If a private party is charged with violating OSHA rules and fined, that party could appeal to the courts if they thought the charges were unfair. Theoretically, the courts could then exercise their legal authority to review the matter, perhaps finding that OSHA overstepped its authority. This scenario is, of course, very much in line with the traditional understanding of checks and balances between the branches.

In facing this responsibility, the courts could overrule the regulator on various grounds. The courts might, for example, find that an agency took too much liberty in writing regulations, exceeding the legislature's mandate. Or, judges might find that an agency, in penalizing the private party, acted arbitrarily—imposing harsh penalties on some while favoring others. Or an agency might simply be found to have done a bad job in applying its own rules to some novel and complicated situation. But as the courts wrestled with such issues over time, a basic question arose: Are the courts really in a position to stand in judgment on the agencies?

This key question would receive a near-definitive answer in a 1984 Supreme Court decision, *Chevron U. S. A. Inc. v. Natural Resources Defense Council, Inc.*[8] *Chevron* was not only a landmark case in administrative law but a source of ongoing controversy. The facts behind it were complex. The starting place was a piece of legislation, the Clean Air Act. Among its provisions, the act required that new industrial projects that created a "stationary source" of pollution must go through a difficult approval process

---

[8] Near definitive for decades, but perhaps not after the summer of 2024. The Supreme Court updated its stance in a 2024 case, *Loper Bright Enterprises v. Raimondo*. The decision's actual effects on administrative law are yet to be understood as of early 2025. However, in commenting on *Loper,* Prof. Vermeule says that there is less there (in terms of overruling *Chevron*) than meets the eye and that the basic forces that led to *Chevron* remain. Among these is the usefulness of "Chevron deference" to judges, who understand the benefits of a division of labor in the case of administrative law. One possible outcome of *Roper,* Vermeule writes, is that it will "be seen to overrule *Chevron*, while also largely preserving *Chevron's* major source of appeal to judges—a way to avoid having to actually do fully independent interpretation of statutory terms that are vague, technical, or both." See his online article *"Chevron* By Any Other Name," https://thenewdigest.substack.com/p/ chevron-by-any-other-name.

to make sure the project will be within regulated levels of emissions. In passing the Clean Air Act, this is what Congress called for.[9]

As the statute was put into effect, however, the definition of "stationary source" came into question. Chevron, the big oil corporation, operated a complex of operations on a single site, with pollution produced by different emitters within it. Was the whole site a stationary source, or was each pollution emitter within the site a stationary source? Chevron's preference was to treat the whole complex as the single source. This would allow the company some flexibility in meeting the emissions standards. So long as the pollution from the whole site was within the limits, the emissions from a specific building or machine on site would not matter. The Environmental Protection Agency (EPA) accepted this reasoning, which, applied elsewhere, would make building new industrial plants easier for corporations such as Chevron and more cost-effective.

Environmentalists, however, took exception to this approach. Treating the whole complex as the source, they argued, was going too easy on Chevron and violated the purpose of the Clean Air Act. So, the Natural Resources Defense Council filed suit against the EPA challenging its interpretation, and in time the case reached the Supreme Court. The Court's job was to settle the specific case at hand, but its decision would go further. It would set a precedent for how much authority regulatory agencies would have and how much oversight of their decisions the judiciary would, as a rule, take on.

In its decision, the Court sided with the EPA, saying the agency had acted appropriately and within its authority. But beyond the

---

[9] NB: The "stationary source" provision actually came with a 1977 amendment to the 1963 Clean Air Act.

specific case, the ruling also established a framework, often called "Chevron deference," which the Court would apply in similar cases. With this framework, the Court acknowledged the authority of regulatory agencies to interpret statutes relatively freely, though within reason. In doing so, the Court acknowledged its own relative incapacity to judge the agencies in light of its lack of expertise when it came to the complex situations those agencies often face. It made no sense for the courts to keep ruling in cases where the agencies would not only be found to have acted reasonably, but where the judges—generalists, like legislators—had all they could handle getting up to speed on the technical intricacies involved. Thus, the *Chevron* decision was significant in terms of the balance of power within government. For the foreseeable future, the judiciary would defer in many cases to the opinion of the agencies, greatly strengthening the administrative state.

Classical liberals might add that *Chevron* strengthened government in relation to the private sector. By deferring to the regulatory agencies, the Court allows for a consolidation of power within the executive branch, weakening intergovernmental checks and balances. The result is a powerful, expansive bureaucracy that, to critics, appears all but invulnerable to external checks.

The Administrative State in Context

Professor Vermeule supports the *Chevron* decision, and by doing so departs again from the originalist position. Unlike many conservative originalists, he supports governmental action in support of broadly shared goals, even if those actions do not pass muster under classical liberal interpretations of the Constitution. As he and co-author Cass Sunstein put it in *Law and Leviathan*: "Consider some of the actual activities of the state. Would people be freer without child labor laws? Without occupational safety laws? Without food safety laws? Without protection from sexual harassment? Without air pollution laws? Without protection against pandemics?"[10] Such goals are worthy, Vermeule believes, and Congress has acted within its powers to establish the agencies to pursue them. Moreover, if government action in such cases is legitimate, some party must hold authority to act and the agencies are in the best position to do so.

To those who see this growth in the agencies' authority as a violation of bedrock constitutional principles, Vermeule takes issue. It is better, he believes, to see the *Chevron* decision as the culmination of a long, difficult process by which the modern administrative state has found its legitimate place within the broader constitutional order. That process unfolded through a decades-long series of Supreme Court cases.[11] Vermeule cites, for example, the *Crowell v. Benson* decision of 1932, which amounted to, in his words, a "colossal effort . . . to achieve a stable accommodation of the claims of law and the imperatives of bureaucratic government. . . ."[12] But the target kept moving as the economy evolved rapidly, so the accommodation proved elusive and needed regular updating before the Court arrived at *Chevron*.

---

[10] Cass Sunstein and Adrian Vermeule, *Law and Leviathan: Redeeming the Administrative State* (Harvard University Press, 2020) 5.

[11] Congress contributed to this process through statutes, the most important of which was the Administrative Procedure Act of 1946.

[12] Adrian Vermeule, *Law's Abnegation: From Law's Empire to the Administrative State* (Harvard University Press, 2016), 12.

The means employed in this process are crucial for Vermeule. The Court, he points out, came to its conclusion in *Chevron* for "valid, lawyerly reasons." Finding room for the modern administrative state involved a major shift in the constitutional order, but it was always understood by those making key decisions along the way that its place must be lawful. The regulatory agencies were never allowed to behave arbitrarily. So, for example, they have their own internal rules, set by Congress,[13] which the agencies must follow. If the agencies failed in this, or failed to meet applicable external laws, the courts could have cracked down. And the courts did scrutinize the agencies over the years. Chevron deference reflected the satisfaction of the courts with the lawfulness of the agencies and their actions, as their efforts at oversight had generally proved. "The main mechanism behind law's *abnegation* [that is, the courts' deference to the administrative agencies] has been a reasoned commitment to reasoned consistency on the part of the legal profession."[14]

But judicial abnegation has profound implications, once again, for our constitutional order. With traditional checks and balances dramatically altered and with the executive branch rising to clear supremacy over the others, the United States now lives in a different constitutional world than the founders imagined. And in Vermeule's eyes we would do well to accept it. At the end of *The Executive Unbound*, he and co-author Eric Posner, addressing fellow scholars, put the matter starkly. They "should no longer view American political life through the Madisonian prism . . ." and "should cease bemoaning the decline of Madisonianism and instead make their

---

[13] Here the Administrative Procedure Act of 1946 is the key legislation.

[14] Vermeule, *Law's Abnegation*, 2.

peace with the new political order."[15] Historical and legal forces have driven this profound change, as Vermeule sees things, but that does not mean that our current order is no longer constitutional.

Vermeule and Legal Positivism

Adrian Vermeule's argument that the "Madisonian" Constitution is no longer viable clearly distances him from the originalist project, but it illuminates only one side of his problem with that doctrine. He also argues that, whatever its usefulness early on, originalism proved all but hollow over time. Explaining why leads to the heart of Vermeule's most important work on constitutionalism and America's constitutional future.

Consider the essence of originalism. In the effort to brake the long train of progressive decisions from the courts, originalists called for the Constitution as it was written to serve as a standard by which to discipline modern jurisprudence. The Constitution is not a bag of tricks from which, through freewheeling interpretation, one might draw whatever conclusions one wants. Instead, as Vermeule puts it, originalists assert that "constitutional meaning was fixed at the time of the Constitution's enactment . . . and that this fixed meaning ought to constrain constitutional practice by judges and other officials."[16]

One of the attractions of this approach was its ideological neutrality. Yes, the originalists tended to be conservative and opposed to the progressive thrust of the courts, but the Constitution itself is essentially procedural and liberal in the sense that it resists the

---

[15] Posner and Vermeule, *The Executive Unbound*, 209.

[16] Adrian Vermeule, *Common Good Constitutionalism* (Polity Press, 2022), 91.

imposition of substantive norms. So originalists could make the public case that their approach—stick to the Constitution—would be impartial in its application.

Yet in Vermeule's eyes, there is a problem here that cannot be resolved, one pointed out by legal philosopher Ronald Dworkin, an arch-progressive. In searching for the original meaning of the Constitution, we cannot avoid actually interpreting its words in light of our own judgment, which is, in a very real sense, what the originalists sought to avoid. To use one familiar example, what do we make of the constitutional ban on "cruel and unusual punishment"? The framers of the Constitution might have had some very specific examples in mind when they wrote those words, but should our notions today be determined by theirs? Recall that those who enacted the Constitution accepted hanging as capital punishment, finding it neither cruel nor unusual. Was it their intention that we could never advance beyond their views? Perhaps they might have been open to the idea of change if, as Vermeule writes, "the advance of knowledge, scientific and moral, showed indisputably that it should be so considered."[17] There is no evidence that the framers of the Constitution intended to prevent this.

So the question of whether to interpret the Constitution strictly by its original meaning, or in a more flexible way, puts originalists on the horns of a dilemma, as Vermeule puts it.[18] Strict readings—hanging is allowable because the founders thought so—might indeed anchor constitutional interpretation. But this approach risks tying us to outmoded positions and leaving us no point of contact

---

[17] Vermeule, *Common Good Constitutionalism*, 97.

[18] Vermeule, *Common Good Constitutionalism*, 95.

with contemporary understandings. On the other hand, interpreting the founders in more flexible terms simply sets us adrift again. In any case, the originalist position fails, under pressure, to give real guidance. As evidence, Vermeule points to the opinion of the Supreme Court in the *Bostock* case, which extended protection against sexual discrimination to homosexual and transgender citizens. As Vermeule notes, the decision was written by "uber-originalist" Justice Gorsuch but did not differ at all from what a progressive judge would have said.[19] And not only was the majority opinion written by an originalist, but one of the dissents, by Justice Kavanaugh, is essentially originalist as well and takes Gorsuch to task for not getting originalism right.[20] If originalism guided both the majority decision and a dissent, what actual use was it as an interpretive tool?

If Vermeule is critical of originalism, however, he finds just as much fault in its old rival, progressivism. In fact, he sees them less as competitors than as twins, and what makes the two similar is that both are examples of legal positivism. That is, both view law as simply what is posited by constitutionally legitimate leaders, irrespective of deeper sources of authority. As the *Stanford Encyclopedia of Philosophy* puts it, positivists believe that a law's legitimacy "depends on social facts and not its merits." Fleshing this out, their definition adds:

> Whether a society has a legal system depends on the
> presence of certain structures of governance, not on the

---

[19] Vermeule, *Common Good Constitutionalism*, 16–17.

[20] Vermeule, *Common Good Constitutionalism*, 106.

extent to which it satisfies the ideals of justice, democracy, or the rule of law. . . . The fact that a policy would
be just, wise, efficient or prudent is never sufficient reason
for thinking that it is actually law, and the fact that it is
unjust, unwise, inefficient or imprudent is never sufficient
reason for doubting it.[21]

To Vermeule, both originalists and progressives see law as independent of substantive truth claims and thus they avoid the demands
of any higher order of the good.

As we have seen, Vermeule, genuinely conservative, has made
common cause with the progressive Cass Sunstein in his defense of
the administrative state. At the same time, however, Vermeule
distrusts the socially liberal aspect of progressivism and the legal
positivism that supports it. Moreover, he does so for the same reason he faults originalism. In essence, it is a-normative; it undermines
the deeper substantive order that law ultimately depends on.

Looking back, this a-normative social liberalism was a hallmark
of the Warren and Burger courts, which did so much to institutional-
ize the rights revolution. The rights claims of individuals, which
impose obligations of acceptance on the broader community, seemed
always (at least to conservatives) to be vindicated by the courts. Vermeule sees something absolutist in this rejection of historically
accepted norms. The thrust of the movement became the liberation
of "the individual will from all unchosen constraints," as he puts it.
More fully, he writes that this form of progressivism

---

[21] "Legal Positivism," *Stanford Encyclopedia of Philosophy*, revised December 17, 2019, https://plato.stanford.edu/entries/legal-positivism/.

treats the law as an instrument that must be bent toward the realization of ever more radical forms of individual liberation and social egalitarianism. This is not to say, of course, that progressivism does not turn enthusiastically to state coercion, but it does so always in the name of liberation of the individual from the unreasoning forces of tradition, authority, and even natural biology.[22]

The coercion Vermeule mentions is important. Overcoming tradition and social norms to achieve liberation takes active effort, given that American culture, like every other in history, is naturally social and tends toward some degree of conformity. To accomplish progressive social ends means breaking down traditional customs, and using law to do so when necessary. This approach has proved fruitful in its way and progressives have had a good deal of success using law to effect social change in ways previously unimaginable. The expansion of marriage to include same-sex couples stands as an example.

It should be emphasized, once again, that the liberationist tendency of progressivism is far from alien to American constitutionalism. The language of the Constitution, the Declaration of Independence, and our political discourse over generations lends itself to private claims to liberty, equality, and rights of all kinds.

However, perhaps in working itself pure the socially liberal strain in American law has grown unbalanced. This would account, as Vermeule sees things, for the crusading quality of contemporary progressivism. It has become a religious belief, he claims provocatively, as much as a political philosophy, and even comes with its

---

[22] Vermeule, *Common Good Constitutionalism*, 121.

own liturgy. That is how Vermeule describes "the repetitive impulse of liberal political theology to celebrate a sacramental moment of overcoming of the unreason and darkness of the traditional past."[23] This political theology comes with "its own cruel sacraments— especially the shaming, and, where possible, the legal punishment of the intolerant or illiberal."[24]

Without any normative order to anchor it, progressivism is driven by its own logic toward "structural instability," always seeking new barriers to tear down. Vermeule writes: "Yesterday the frontier was divorce, contraception and abortion; then it became same-sex marriage; today it is transgenderism; tomorrow it may be polygamy, consensual adult incest, or who knows what." This open-endedness, Vermeule claims, is part of the deep appeal for progressives, always searching for new ways to extend the frontiers of their own open-mindedness. "[T]he essential thing is that the new issue provokes opposition from the forces of reaction, who may then be conquered in a public and dramatic fashion by the political mobilization of liberal forces."[25] This sort of drama, familiar from the news, satisfies some deep need for those who orchestrate and pursue it, as he sees things, but is also profoundly at odds with the good of society as a whole.

Law, Order, and Reality

If we unpack Vermeule's problem with positivist law, we see where his legal views lead. Severed from deeper, substantive norms, law

---

[23] Vermeule, *Common Good Constitutionalism*, 119.

[24] Adrian Vermeule, "A Christian Strategy," in *First Things*, November, 2017, https://www.firstthings.com/article/2017/11/a-christian-strategy.

[25] Vermeule, "A Christian Strategy," 2017.

becomes "instrumentalized," that is it becomes merely a tool to achieve goals preferred by a given politically organized group. The key reference point is what the group wants. But law used as a tool in this way is, in Vermeule's eyes, not really law at all. As he writes: "To instrumentalize the law is to use it as a tool for extrinsic ends that warp its true nature."[26]

This is a notion pregnant with meaning. If law has a "true nature" that can be warped by using it to achieve "extrinsic" purposes, then law must relate to some intrinsic, objective reality that transcends those purposes. If we pass laws that violate the order of that reality, they lose legitimacy. Moreover, if we try to live by those disordered laws, we will incur some very real penalty for that violation. If the law has a true nature, and our laws must be in tune with that transcendent reality, we cannot see ourselves as clearly apart from that order. We live in relation to it, whether we violate that reality or live in harmony with it. In making this case for natural law, Vermeule understands full well that this view is in tension with the liberal impulses of our constitutional system and its resistance to notions of preexisting order.

But the reality of a natural order is central to Vermeule's constitutional thought, which aims to shift the balance of American law away from its most liberal interpretations and toward an accord with that order. One place where we can see an example of this is his insistence that humans are fundamentally social creatures, and in a more profound way than the social contract theory conveys. Thus, politics, properly speaking, has to do with the well-being of the *polis,* the people as a society. Accordingly, Vermeule writes that "law

---

[26] Vermeule, *Common Good Constitutionalism*, 120.

should be seen as a reasoned ordering of the common good . . . that promotes the good of law's subjects *as members of a flourishing community. . . .*"[27] [Italics added.]

The good of a flourishing community fulfills us as persons in ways that a life of individual achievement cannot. To make this point, Vermeule compares the common good to the good of a football team. When the team plays well, it is a group achievement; when we participate on a successful team, we achieve something that we cannot do alone; and when we contribute to a team effort, it satisfies something people crave and that individual achievements cannot. In a parallel vein, the aim of politics is not just to provide the conditions that make it possible to flourish as individuals, achieving personal prosperity or other accomplishments. Instead, "the highest felicity in the temporal sphere is itself the common life of the well-ordered community, which includes those other foundational goods but transcends them as well."[28]

To further clarify what the common good amounts to, Vermeule offers three antitypes. First is *aggregation*, or the view that the sum of private successes will add up to the well-being of the whole. For Vermeule, private welfare is good, but insufficient. "To be sure, it is important that the common good is also good for individuals, indeed their highest good, but the common good is not produced by the summation of individual goods."[29]

[27] Vermeule, *Common Good Constitutionalism*, 1.

[28] Vermeule, *Common Good Constitutionalism*, 28.

[29] Vermeule, *Common Good Constitutionalism*, 26.

A second antitype of the common good is what Vermeule describes as *tyranny and faction*, or rule for private benefit.[30] The contrast with the common good is obvious here: People who use government for private or factional gain degrade the shared endeavor that rightful rule fosters. As Vermeule makes clear, the gains sought through tyranny or faction might be individual, as would be the case with a leader who enriches him- or herself at the public's expense. However, this type of misrule could also include the enrichment of specific groups. For example, in classical political theory the difference between aristocracy and oligarchy is the difference between public interest (which aristocrats seek) and the self-interest of the rich (which the oligarchs seek).

A third antitype is *monstrous government*, whose defining characteristic is "a multiplicity of quasi-independent private tyrants dominating a weak public authority."[31] Here we might imagine the warlords of old, who challenge and destabilize a legitimate king. But we might also think of today's high-tech companies, which hold so much power over the flow of information in the public sphere. In any case, the harm done by powerful, self-interested private actors does violence to the common good, and the threat they pose demands strength in government to counteract their machinations. Here we might also recall the growth of government's powers during the first half of the twentieth century as a response to the rise of big business. Vermeule sees no problem with that, and one key theme of his writings is the need for strong government, especially a strong executive, to act on behalf of the common good. Among

---

[30] Vermeule, *Common Good Constitutionalism*, 26–27.

[31] Vermeule, *Common Good Constitutionalism*, 27.

his favorite maxims is one from a Spanish thinker, Ricardo Calleja: *imperare aude*—"dare to command."[32]

American Law and the Classical Legal Tradition
There is a hitch here. The idea of an empowered chief executive who dares to command is the stuff of American political night-mares. From the start we have been wary of concentrated power in government, a fact that Vermeule understands full well. It is no coincidence that our founding story has a royal villain, King George III, and Americans have long been unusually susceptible to *tyran-nophobia*, as Vermeule and Posner put it in *The Executive Unbound*. However, Vermeule encourages readers to step outside the well-worn ruts of this very American taboo and consider the possibility that we might learn something from beyond our own political mythologies. As a student of classical culture and law, as well as Chinese thought, he understands that the United States is not history's sole example of a large, diverse, political state. And we could surely use the perspective found by taking seriously the experiences of other nations and empires.

Especially useful in Vermeule's eyes is the long history of Western legal thought, stretching back through the medieval period to the Roman, a legacy that he calls the *classical legal tradition*. For Vermeule, a central lesson from the study of classi-cal and medieval law is the underlying acceptance throughout this history of natural law. That is, law grounded in an order from which, and within which, society takes shape. Law makes no sense without this deeper order.

---

[32] Vermeule, *Common Good Constitutionalism*, 71.

Here it is useful, Vermeule points out, to think of law as having two dimensions. There is the written law, what we find in the books of any political state. To use a term from Roman law, this is *lex*. What gives lex its life, however, is a deeper law, *ius,* or "the right." As Vermeule puts it, *"Ius* is the overall body of law generally, including and subsuming lex, but transcending it and containing general principles of jurisprudence and legal justice."[33] Vermeule quotes the Roman jurist Ulpian, who touched on the essence of *ius* in these terms: "to live honorably, not to harm any other person, to render to each his own."[34] *Ius* gives life to lex, and when lex departs from the principles of *ius* it loses legitimacy. Glossing Thomas Aquinas, Vermeule writes that "a law that is out of step with natural justice . . . does not simply become no-law, as though it had never been created; rather, it results in a perverted caricature of law."[35]

While lex cannot violate *ius* without losing its legitimacy, the universal principles of *ius* must be received or translated into concrete laws by given political societies. Different societies will do so in their own ways, and the variations among them are perfectly natural and legitimate. Interestingly, Vermeule considers American democracy in this light. Can democracy provide a legitimate basis for governance? And is democracy the only legitimate basis? Yes and no, in very brief. He quotes Aquinas here again, who, while he thought kingship was the best form of government, also wrote that "all should have some share in the government; for an arrangement of this kind secures the peace of the people, and all men love and

---

[33] Vermeule, *Common Good Constitutionalism*, 4.

[34] Vermeule, *Common Good Constitutionalism*, 30.

[35] Vermeule, *Common Good Constitutionalism*, 120.

defend it."[36] At the same time, however, what gives a government
its legitimacy is its relation to *ius* and various forms of government
can meet that standard. As Vermeule writes, "Democracy—in the
modern sense of mass electoral democracy—has no special privilege
in this regard."[37]

To drill down in the case of the United States, we must ask how
its constitutional order relates to *ius*. Crucially, political liberalism is
defined by its rejection of traditional political orders, and, as we have
seen, the US Constitution is in key respects a liberal document. Given
this, it seems only natural that a good deal of law in the United States
reflects the basic assumptions of political liberalism: the freedom
from traditional hierarchies and imposed systems of order, as seen
in First Amendment, for example. But, Vermeule writes, "just
because *ius* is lost to view does not mean that it has been purged from
American law—far from it." Law in this nation always has kept some
contact with basic notions of the right, as it must.

Classical Law in the US: Prior to the Constitution

As an example, Vermeule points to the police powers, the power of
government to act "for protection of the health, morals, and safety
of the people," as the Supreme Court defined it.[38] To Vermeule, the
police power is not just a dry, legalistic justification of government
action, but something deeper. The police power not only existed prior
to the US Constitution but necessarily exists wherever government

---

[36] Vermeule, *Common Good Constitutionalism*, 48.

[37] Vermeule, *Common Good Constitutionalism*, 47.

[38] The phrasing came in the 1870 decision *Mugler v. Kansas,* 123 U.S. 623 (1887).

itself does. In the 1877 case *Munn v. Illinois*, the Supreme Court offered these thoughts on its universality:

> When one becomes a member of society, he necessarily parts with some rights or privileges which, as an individual not affected by his relations to others, he might retain. "A body politic," as aptly defined by the preamble of the constitution of Massachusetts, "is a social compact by which the whole people covenants with each citizen, and each citizen with the whole people, that all shall be governed by certain laws for the common good."

As the *Munn* decision also states, and Vermeule also quotes, the police powers "are nothing more or less than the powers of government inherent in every sovereignty . . . that is to say, . . . the power to govern men and things."[39]

Thus the police power is more fundamental to the law than the Constitution and trumps it, at least if that power is in tune with *ius*. To further illustrate, Vermeule points to a Supreme Court ruling from 1936, *The United States v. Curtiss-Wright Export Corp.*, which he describes as a model decision.[40] The case concerned a law passed by Congress, which effectively banned arms sales to foreign governments involved in a South American conflict. Aviation manufacturer Curtiss-Wright, which sold fighter planes to Bolivia, claimed the right to do so despite the law, arguing that the Constitution did not grant

---

[39] *Munn v. Illinois*, 94 U.S. 113 (1887).

[40] Adrian Vermeule, "The Union Existed Before the Constitution," *Ius et Iusticium*, Oct. 6, 2020. https://iusetiustitium.com/the-union-existed-before-the-constitution/.

Congress the power to outlaw those sales. So the question for the Court was who was right: Did the government have the legitimate power to stop those sales, or did the Constitution prevent such interference in the free market?

The Court decided against Curtiss-Wright and in support of Congress's ban, and its decision rested largely on natural law foundations. Essentially, the Court had to grapple with the question of where the sovereign power of the nation came from and whether it was limited by the terms of the Constitution. It took as a starting point that this power has a natural existence inherent in every nation. "A political society cannot endure without a supreme will somewhere. Sovereignty is never held in suspense," the Court wrote. In the case of the United States, the sovereign power came with independence and so existed before the Constitution was written. Thus, the Constitution did not create American sovereignty. Indeed, not only are there "pre-Constitutional" powers inherent in American government, but the *Curtiss-Wright* decision states that the American Union itself "existed before the Constitution," which Vermeule says "may be one of the most consequential [statements] ever to appear in the United States Reports" [the official record of Supreme Court decisions].[41] This is so because the statement points to a reality more fundamental than the Constitution, or any legal text.

What *Curtiss-Wright* points to is the enduring presence of natural law. Whatever the founders' pretense of looking forward to a *novus ordo seclorum*,[42] they were steeped in traditions that

---

[41] Vermeule, "The Union," 2020.

[42] Or "new order of the ages."

reflected natural law, which, moreover, have been present in our legal system ever since. "The principles of the classical legal tradition are our own principles, written into our own traditions," as Vermeule writes. "Right from the beginning, long before the Constitution of 1789 was written, the classical legal tradition structured and suffused our law."[43] The originalists miss this if they focus solely on the written Constitution as their touchstone; the progressives miss it as they focus on the positive law and the hope that they can create new social worlds through it.

Applying the Classical Legal Tradition

In his book on common good constitutionalism, Vermeule discusses a number of contemporary challenges where classical legal thought can be applied, offering solutions wholly apart from the "exhausted" arguments between originalism and progressivism.[44] Among them, there is no area where the challenge of applying classical tradition to our civic life is more difficult than that of personal rights. As legal philosopher Ronald Dworkin put it, the concept of individual rights is for Americans "the zodiac sign under which their country was born,"[45] and both originalists and progressives canonize these rights in their different ways. By contrast, however, the classical tradition, or common good constitutionalism, will demand that Americans look at individual rights in a light we are unaccustomed to.

---

[43] Vermeule, *Common Good Constitutionalism*, 53.

[44] Vermeule, "The Union," 2020.

[45] Ronald Dworkin, *A Matter of Principle* (Harvard University Press, 1986), 31.

Rights and the Classical Tradition

Vermeule embraces this change of perspective. While the classical tradition does protect rights, it conceives of them in a way different from the liberal tradition, grounding them in different soil. "The crucial distinction," he writes, "between the classical and modern conceptions involves the question of *justification* of rights." In liberal discourse, the justification centers on personal autonomy, generally assumed to be a good in and of itself, resistant as liberalism is to the concept of a preexisting, authoritative order. In the classical tradition, the justification relates to the common good, where, Vermeule reminds us, the individual finds his or her deepest satisfaction. Thus, taking freedom of speech as an example, the classical tradition defends the right to free speech for what it contributes to communal discourse, and not because individuals ought to be able to say whatever they please.[46]

To illustrate the difference, Vermeule points to the Supreme Court's 2002 decision in *Ashcroft v. Free Speech Coalition*, which, he says, "only a Court ideologically oblivious to the common good could have issued."[47] The case involved the interpretation of the Child Pornography Prevention Act of 1996, legislation that banned the images of minors apparently engaged in sexual activity, even if the images were not of actual children. This would include cases where a young-looking adult portrays a child, for example, or where technology allows for the creation of such images without any actual person being photographed or filmed.

---

[46] Vermeule, *Common Good Constitutionalism*, 165.

[47] Vermeule, *Common Good Constitutionalism*, 165.

Cautious about infringing on individual rights, the Court struck down key provisions of the act, finding that the legislation was "overbroad" and that it would prohibit speech that the Court had previously ruled acceptable. The decision also reiterated what the earlier Court had clearly stated: "[T]he fact that society may find speech offensive is not a sufficient reason for suppressing it." In addition, raising the question of harm, the Court claimed that producing pornography of this sort involves "no crime and creates no victims by its production."[48]

Vermeule finds this verdict ludicrous. This is largely so because it failed to address the real damage done by the speech in question, damage that common good thinking is attuned to. As to the claim that no one is harmed, Vermeule writes: "The victim is both, simultaneously, the person watching and the whole polity. Child pornography tears at the very fabric of natural human order in ways that cannot be accounted for in a narrow calculus of immediate harms in production or use."[49]

Nor does he accept previous rulings on obscenity that *Ashcroft v. Free Speech Coalition* cites. Where they concern pornography, our permissive laws have shallow legal roots, being "a product of the free speech revolution of the 1960s and 1970s". . . ."[50] And this legal permissiveness amounts to an abdication of a key responsibility, present in the standard formulation of the police powers: to protect the moral well-being of the community, as well as its safety, health, and welfare. "Public prohibition of pornography is a form

---

[48] *Ashcroft v. Free Speech Coalition*, 535 U.S. 234 (2002).

[49] Vermeule, *Common Good Constitutionalism*, 171.

[50] Vermeule, *Common Good Constitutionalism*, 171.

of environmcntalism for morals, and should be left to the reasonable determination of public authorities. . . ."[51]

The Environment

Common good constitutionalism, Vermeule believes, must also apply
to environmental concerns as we ordinarily conceive them. Here, as
in the case of free speech, the conceptual framework differs from
what most Americans will find in our public discourse. In an essay
on environmental law, "The Party of Nature," Vermeule criticizes
both "left" and "right." Progressives, he thinks, rightly discount the
strongest claims of property rights when calling for environmental
regulations: Individual property rights are valuable, but they do not
trump the health of the environment, which is so obviously important
to the common good. But Vermeule sees in progressivism more generally an anti-natural attitude in other respects. By emphasizing a radical form of human autonomy in other spheres, progressives fail to
see our profound connectedness to the created world. For example,
the progressive often "sees the human body itself as a plastic mold
to be shaped through surgical modification into whatever shape or
age or gender the body's Gnostic inhabitant fancies. . . ." In this
respect, progressives are "radically libertarian with respect to the
relationship between nature and the human person," while at the
same time they are "technocratic and statist with respect to a broad
range of what are commonly seen as 'environmental issues.'"[52]

The right, to Vermeule, offers a mirror image of the left's views.
It is more likely to oppose the "refashioning" of the human body,

[51] Vermeule, *Common Good Constitutionalism*, 171.

[52] Adrian Vermeule, "The Party of Nature" *Postliberal Order*, December 7,
2021, https://postliberalorder.substack.com/p/the-party-of-nature.

but to the degree it embraces economic liberalism it might also resist state actions to protect endangered species, control pollution in some cases, and reduce human effects on the climate. Like the left, it embraces "a dualistic view of the relationship between man and nature, one that sees man not as an indwelling steward of nature, but as an instrumental master of it."[53]

In opposition to both left and right, as he sees matters, Vermeule proposes a more holistic approach to environmental concerns. He encourages a "Party of Nature," that "believes plants, animals, the human body, the landscape, and even the climate all have real and objective inner integrity, unchosen by man, that man is obligated to respect, tend, and if necessary repair."[54]

This framework opens the door to a great deal of state action on the environmental front. As Vermeule puts it, common good constitutionalism as it relates to the environment supports an "expansive version of the 'public trust' doctrine," by which the state has both the right and duty to protect the environment. We have seen Vermeule's confidence in the regulatory state, and agencies such as the EPA would presumably have a major role in this work. But even more essential to his view is a change in the way we relate to the environment—a demotion of pure individualism and a reimagining of our place within the created world.

Federalism, Subsidiarity, and the Common Good

Common good constitutionalism centers on the idea of shared interests and the common destiny of a political community as a

---

[53] Vermeule, "The Party of Nature," 2021.

[54] Vermeule, "The Party of Nature," 2021.

community. Matching that, a common good approach is also consistent with a unity and coherence in government.

Supporting this, Adrian Vermeule often finds himself in tension with the liberal aspects of our constitutional system. A crucial example is federalism, or the division of power among the different levels of government—national, state, and local. This is one of the most basic ways in which power is diffused, rather than concentrated, in the American system. The legitimate claim of states, cities, counties, and towns to some share of governmental power is naturally at odds with the tendency of common good thinking to centralize power and hold it accountable to the universal standards of *ius*.

For Vermeule federalism is related to the doctrine of *subsidiarity*, a term associated with Catholic social thought. Often, as Vermeule points out, subsidiarity is defined as a "negative limitation," a strong preference for government to meet responsibilities at lower rather than higher levels. If a problem can be solved by local authorities, for example, it should be, with state or national government standing aside. But subsidiarity is also consistent with neighborhoods and families, as well as other non-governmental institutions, taking up key responsibilities for ordering society.

This take on subsidiarity is not wrong in Vermeule's eyes, but incomplete. To explain, he looks to the term's historical roots, which lead back to Roman military doctrines. Rome's tacticians, in planning for battle, held a force in reserve called a *subsidium*. If the front line weakened in a particular place during battle, the subsidium could be sent in to shore it up. From this, Vermeule draws parallels for political subsidiarity. One is that subsidiarity implies a superior center of power, from which support can come.

The logic is one of safeguarding, of extraordinary power and responsibility to preserve, protect, and restore the proper functioning and competences of subsidiary jurisdictions and authorities.[55]

Clear from the context, the subsidium, dispatched from the central command, must be powerful enough for the tactic to work. To return from military history to governance, Vermeule quotes Catholic jurist Johannes Messner on the balance of power between lower and higher levels of government when the front lines weaken. "Where the will to moral responsibility in a society shrinks, . . . the common good function [of the state] expands. . . . In such cases, even dictatorship may be compatible with the principle of subsidiarity."[56] To clarify, Vermeule is confident that Messner is speaking about the ancient Roman tradition of dictatorship, with its constitutionally "cabined" authority, and not of modern unaccountable, strongman-type dictators.

While there are obvious parallels between the doctrine of subsidiarity and American federalism, they differ in their philosophical underpinnings. Among the differences is the one between the clear hierarchy of powers assumed by subsidiarity and the less clear tradition of divided sovereignty under federalism. While a strong American doctrine of state sovereignty suffered a decisive setback with the Civil War, there remain areas where the states retain a primacy in policymaking. This primacy includes the application of police powers in many cases. Moreover, the final limits of federal authority over

---

[55] Vermeule, *Common Good Constitutionalism*, 156.

[56] Vermeule, *Common Good Constitutionalism*, 157.

the states have not been perfectly mapped, and perhaps cannot be given the push and pull of historical circumstances.[57] The *Dobbs* ruling, which returned power over the regulation of abortion to the states after decades of national protection under *Roe v. Wade,* is one example of this.

Consistent with his preference for unitary authority and belief in a genuinely *common* good, Vermeule is wary of the divided sovereignty that comes with American federalism. The claim that state sovereignty limits federal jurisdiction is, in his words, "pernicious." Federalism is best understood as a "principle of respect and comity," grounded in the Constitution but not as setting hard limits on the ultimate authority of the national government.[58] As to those potential hard limits, Vermeule sees them as dangerous. Rather than setting such limits on a nation's highest authority, better to allow for vigorous centralized power to be used when necessary. Thus, a well-conceived constitution might encourage cities and states to bear real responsibilities for governing themselves—subsidiarity calls for as much—but it will also allow for the overriding power of the truer sovereign, the national government, when circumstances demand it.[59]

Where We Are: The Arc of American Law
Although professors Vermeule, Epstein, and Sunstein disagree on a great deal, they do share the understanding that American law shifted dramatically during the course of the twentieth century. For Epstein, the turn amounted to a dangerous rejection of traditional

---

[57] In recent years, for example, the state of Texas has tested its power in relation to the federal government in a confrontation over border security.

[58] Vermeule, *Common Good Constitutionalism*, 158.

[59] Vermeule, *Common Good Constitutionalism*, 160–164.

constitutional restraints on government. For Sunstein, the change was a welcome revolution, opening the door to needed reform, a movement that is still unfolding today.

Vermeule sees the shift in twentieth-century law in a different light. What is crucial is that during the years between World War I and World War II, roughly speaking, legal positivism drove out a good deal of the classical legal tradition, with its affinity for natural law. This amounted, in his words, to "an ill-considered fit of rebellion," one in which we continue to this day.

Seen from Vermeule's perspective, however, this rebellion is untenable. However much liberal legal theorists, left or right, downplay the notion that we are bound by any order except what we decide upon, the actual practice of law still depends on such a preexisting order. As Vermeule puts it, "classical law and natural law . . . could be officially denied or said to be irrelevant, but . . . could never be eradicated from the judicial mind."[60] Trying to do so renders the idea of law itself incoherent.

But our problem today is that theory and reality diverge not only in law, but more broadly. At least in rhetoric, American liberalism embraces a live-and-let-live society, where commitments to prescribed standards are minimal. Looking around, however, Vermeule sees something entirely different at work. "[A]lmost no one in America in 2024, barring a few professors and elderly journalists, is really a political liberal in the sense theorists advocate." Instead, public life is dominated by a "comprehensive and perfectionist version of liberalism" that aggressively pursues its

---

[60] Adrian Vermeule, "Why I Lost Interest in the Liberalism Debate: On Science-Fictional Political Theory," *The New Digest*, February 3, 2024, https://thenewdigest.substack.com/p/why-i-lost-interest-in-the-liberalism.

liberationist project.[61] In other words, perfectionist liberalism will not live side by side with more conservative elements in society, but will instead act to drive them out.

Progressives are not alone in this ruthlessness. They are joined by the political right in their "thirst to prosecute their enemies," and both sides, right and left, "tremble eagerly in the hope of making their respective comprehensive views the master-view, the dominant view. . . ." as Vermeule puts it. This is not a temporary quirk in American political life. It is, practically speaking, inevitable, since people universally hope to live according to a shared concept of what is right. "Political liberalism, even if possible in principle, simply turned out to be unsustainable as a matter of the deep facts of human anthropology and human psychology."[62]

This divergence of theory—or national mythology—and practice leaves us in an unsustainable situation. Along the arc of American law, Vermeule believes, we have come to a point not only of exhaustion, but of instability. It is a situation where "the originalist party denies that law is the art of justice at all, and the Progressive Party denies that justice transcends the satisfaction of the individual will," and this "rubs against the grain of reality."[63] We need renewal, but more specifically we need a more deeply realistic constitutionalism, one that would

> take as its starting point substantive moral principles that conduce to the common good. . . . These principles

---

[61] Vermeule, "Why I Lost Interest in the Liberalism Debate," 2024.

[62] Vermeule, "Why I Lost Interest in the Liberalism Debate," 2024.

[63] Vermeule, *Common Good Constitutionalism,* 184.

include respect for the authority of rule and of rulers; respect for the hierarchies needed for society to function; solidarity within and among families, social groups, and workers' unions, trade associations, and professions; appropriate solidarity, or respect for the legitimate roles of public bodies and associations at all levels of government and society; and a candid willingness to "legislate morality"—indeed, a recognition that all legislation is necessarily founded on some substantive conception of morality, and that the promotion of morality is a core and legitimate function of authority. Such principles promote the common good and make for a just and well-ordered society.[64]

Finally, Vermeule, while understanding that this is a tall order, sees institutional means already in place for such an ambitious political reformation. The means are found in the powerful executive and its administrative agencies. Rather than scuttling what we have built, we should work with these existing institutions, repurposing them where need be, to "transform the decaying regime from within. . . . The vast bureaucracy created by liberalism in pursuit of a mirage of depoliticized governance may, by the invisible hand of Providence, be turned to new ends, becoming the great instrument with which to restore a substantive politics of the good."[65]

---

[64] Adrian Vermeule, "Beyond Originalism," *The Atlantic*, March 31, 2020.

[65] Adrian Vermeule, "Integration from Within," *American Affairs*, February 20, 2018.

Conclusion

A LONG CONSTITUTIONAL MOMENT

It is something of a bragging point for the United States that our Constitution is the "world's longest surviving written charter of government," as the US Senate's official website puts it.[1] While that is true enough, one of the themes of this book is that the Constitution has not exactly survived, at least not in its original form. As time has passed, it has been interpreted in new enough ways that our government today is not only vastly more expansive than anything the founders could have imagined, but our jurisprudence is now, as Richard Epstein might point out, inimical in certain key respects to the founding vision.

Whether this is cause for concern or not, opinions differ. Both Cass Sunstein and Adrian Vermeule (in their differing ways) see the evolution of American government during the twentieth century as entirely acceptable, even a positive good, given the historical

---

[1] United States Senate, "Constitution of the United States," https://www.senate.gov/about/origins-foundations/senate-and-constitution/constitution.htm.

circumstances. But the differences between the scholars featured in these pages points to another theme of the book: the deep divisions of opinion among leading legal thinkers about the meaning of the Constitution, as, indeed, similarly deep divisions exist among the people themselves. In this regard, it seems significant that each of the three scholars we have focused on can lay claim to being in the mainstream of our constitutional tradition: Epstein, with his fidelity to the original vision of the Constitution; Sunstein, writing from the heart of the (nearly) dominant progressive movement of recent decades; and Vermeule advocating the classical tradition, which encompasses American constitutionalism, but extends much farther back in Western history.

Of course, seeing each of these scholars, who differ so substantially, as part of an American mainstream raises the question: Where is this mainstream actually and what does it amount to? Which invites other questions at least as challenging. If we look for a source of legitimacy for our laws and our order, where do we find it? If it is hard to find the mainstream, can we even say that there is any source of legitimacy for the system taken as a whole? In more harmonious times, we could ignore such questions, but concerns with deep-seated political divisions and social deterioration today make it necessary to look hard at the foundation of our constitutional order and to question its strength. By way of review, here, in very brief form, are the positions of our three scholars as they relate not only to legitimacy, but also our constitutional future.

Richard Epstein
For legitimacy, look to the Constitution and accept its original philosophy, which is to say, its classical liberalism. When we have

departed from that approach, in breaking down property rights, for instance, or in launching governmental efforts to reengineer society, we end up making ourselves poorer and more faction-ridden. Such deviations from a principled, classically liberal reading of the Constitution have also left the legitimacy of the current system cloudier and weaker. "No constitution could hope to survive if not driven by some general, guiding theory," Epstein writes in *The Classical Liberal Constitution*.[2] And if we want to repair the damage done to our system over the last hundred years, he is clear about how to go about it: "The blunt truth is that a strong embrace of the classical liberal constitution offers the only sure path to rejuvenation of America's constitutional and political institutions."[3]

Cass Sunstein

To interpret America's constitutional order strictly by classical liberal standards is far too constraining, tying government's hands as we face manifold economic and social challenges. In any case, while maintaining constitutional consistency over time has its place, Sunstein emphasizes the need for social transformation and the necessity of the Constitution to foster that. This commitment to change can be seen in his ideal of deliberative democracy. Real democracy must promote reason and reflection through deliberation; that deliberation must be open to diverse views; and citizens must not take preexisting norms as natural or unalterable. "A central point of deliberation, in the private and public domains, is

---

[2] Richard A. Epstein, *The Classical Liberal Constitution: The Uncertain Quest for Limited Government* (Harvard University Press, 2014), 582.

[3] Epstein, *The Classical Liberal Constitution*, 583.

to shape both preferences and beliefs, and frequently to alter them, by subjecting them to reasoned arguments."[4]

Sunstein's often adversarial relation to tradition is on display here and it relates to the rightfulness of American governance as a whole. To ensure the well-being of our nation, we must search ourselves, through free and vigorous discourse, sustaining a critique where success is measured by the full acceptance of all members of society, with none relegated to second-class status. And here we return to something Sunstein wrote back in the early 1990s: "[W]e might even define political truth as the outcome of this deliberative process. . . ."[5]

Adrian Vermeule

In seeking the sources of constitutional legitimacy, consider where it *cannot* be found. For this, recall Vermeule's take on America's turn toward legal positivism early in the twentieth century, which he called "an ill-considered fit of rebellion."[6] The use of *rebellion* here suggests that positivism amounts to an uprising against rightful authority. Recall that according to positivism, law is legitimate so long as it is passed according to an accepted procedure; it needs no other basis than that. But is law really self-legitimating in this way? To Vermeule, the answer is no. Prior to any procedure, any constitution, there is an order of justice in nature—*ius*—and any law that runs counter to that order is illegitimate, whether correct procedures, even democratic ones, are followed or not.

---

[4] Sunstein, *Designing Democracy*, 6–8.

[5] Sunstein, *Democracy and the Problem of Free Speech*, 19.

[6] Vermeule, *Common Good Constitutionalism*, 180.

Severed from deeper sources of the good, a legal and political system not only lacks legitimacy, it grows ever more lifeless. In a public conversation with entrepreneur Peter Thiel, Vermeule commented, with grim humor, on what he sees as the deepening crisis of our current political state of affairs: "We feel quite stuck in a kind of gerontocratic boomer-liberal regime that seems to go on indefinitely. . . [P]erhaps boomer liberalism can turn itself into a kind of immortal vampirism, but I'm not so convinced yet. I think nature will catch up with it, though it's taking a shockingly long time."[7]

Any hope for a return to good constitutional health starts by ending the positivist rebellion and re-embracing *ius* as the ultimate source of our laws. Fortunately, we can draw on "our own magnificent legal heritage"[8] to guide us, the historical body of laws and legal reflection in which *ius* has its rightful place. If we want to right the ship of state, this is where to start. "The best way to go forward is to look backward for inspiration. A revival and adaptation of the classical law, translated into today's circumstances, is the only way to restore the integrity of our law and of our legal traditions."[9]

Liberty and Order Revisited

Looking back over the alarming events of recent years—COVID-19, the riots that followed George Floyd's death, the January 6 mob takeover of Congress, the attempted assassination of Donald

---

[7] Peter Thiel, "Keynote Address: The Conservative and Republican Student Conference," *The Harvard Salient,* video presentation, YouTube. See the discussion around 39:00–45:00, https://www.youtube.com/ watch?v=euzxpbBOju8.

[8] Vermeule, *Common Good Constitutionalism,* 180.

[9] Vermeule, *Common Good Constitutionalism,* 183.

Trump, and more—reveals how divided Americans have become. Events were understood in nearly diametrically opposed ways by differing blocs, as were the appropriate responses to those events. As a fitting windup to this period of dissension, the 2024 presidential campaign featured high-ranking Democrats attacking their Republican opponent and his supporters as fascist, while prominent backers of Donald Trump also scorched the earth, rhetorically speaking. Elon Musk, campaigning for Trump, asserted that if Democrats won it would usher in an era of one-party rule and political ruin: "Very few Americans realize that if Trump is NOT elected, this will be the last election."[10] We might be forgiven for thinking that we crossed some constitutional point of no return in the early 2020s. And whatever happens in coming years, it will not look like recent decades.

This situation was anticipated by a celebrated historian of law, Harold J. Berman, writing decades ago. As a historian, he took a long view of matters, almost like that of a geologist. Berman analyzed the last thousand years of Western legal history, searching out its patterns of change, especially in his magisterial books on law and revolution. In 1985, he applied this broad perspective in an address to the Boston College Law School, later published with the title "The Crisis of Legal Education in America." For Berman, the crisis had nothing to do with the intelligence of students or faculty, nor about any unwillingness of law students to serve the public interest. Instead, the crisis lay in attitudes toward law itself. "We have been overwhelmed by the belief that law is politics—and politics in a rather

---

[10] Sarah Fortinsky, "Elon Musk: Voting for Trump the 'only way to save democracy,'" *The Hill,* September 30, 2015; https://thehill.com/policy/technology/4906822-elon-musk-donald-trump-democracy/.

narrow sense . . . namely, domination." To Berman, law was no longer seen as serving a higher purpose that transcended rival factions. Instead, law was increasingly seen only as "a pragmatic device, an instrument, used by those in power to accomplish their will."[11] Not that law shouldn't serve pragmatic ends; as Berman fully understood, it must. But what he found missing from the reigning view of the law was an understanding that it is "rooted in something bigger than the people who hand it down. . . ."[12]

This book opened with a question about "constitutional moments," points of political inflection, and whether we are facing one today. I believe we are facing such a moment, and it relates to Harold Berman's concern about the loss of some sense of order that in the past lent a critical degree of coherence to our otherwise enormously diverse American population. And the crisis we face will not be solved by any definitive act—an election, for instance, or an act of Congress. Berman saw our loss of a shared faith in an overarching order as consistent with broader cultural changes. "Obviously, the problems . . . are part of a much larger movement of history. The traditional Western beliefs in the structural integrity of the law, its ongoingness, its religious roots, and its transcendent qualities, are not only disappearing from the minds of law teachers and law students, but also from the consciousness of the vast majority of citizens, of the people as a whole. . . ."[13] If so, the challenges we face can hardly be solved by any political silver

---

[11] Harold J. Berman, "The Crisis of Legal Education in America," *Faith and Order: The Reconciliation of Law and Religion* (Eerdmans Publishing, 1993), 334.

[12] Berman, "The Crisis of Legal Education in America," 334.

[13] Berman, "The Crisis of Legal Education in America," 338.

bullet. Our constitutional "moment" might last a very long time, perhaps many decades.

A Path to the Future?

Berman, however, offers something of a roadmap for finding our way beyond the current impasse, and his suggestion relates to a question raised in the introduction to this book. Are the approaches to the Constitution explored in the preceding chapters irreconcilable? Generally, the differing views of our three scholars have been treated as not only distinct, but as antithetical. Follow Richard Epstein's anti-statist recommendations and we will find ourselves in a very different place than if we followed Adrian Vermeule's common good constitutionalism. Or, to take another example, seeing law through a positivist lens, whereby law's legitimacy depends solely on the will of the sovereign, is at odds with any sort of natural law.

For Berman, however, we should look again at the assumption of irreconcilability and learn to overcome it. If a certain logic points toward the incompatibility of constitutional viewpoints, a different perspective and a deeper logic might allow their reconciliation. For example, instead of seeing positivism and natural law as simple opponents, we can see each as not only legitimate in its way, but as necessary to a healthy constitutional system. If laws are simply "posited," as Berman puts it, without reference to deeper notions of what is right by nature, those laws run the risk of being arbitrary and, in their shallowness, losing the resonant respect of constituents. Yet the deeper moral meanings found in natural law must be interpreted and adapted to the contingencies of place and time, which positivism allows. What is needed, Berman suggests, is for the two to "interpenetrate," rather than overshadow or cancel, one another. [14] Likewise with liberty and order; they need not stand in rigid opposition, but can inform and enrich each other.

Yet the tendency has been for differing schools of interpretation to assert their primacy over each other, a disposition that Berman associates historically with the Enlightenment. Prior to the eighteenth century, differing theories were seen not as separate, competing schools, but as "complementary perspectives on law," [15] and this is what we should return to. One reason we have trouble seeing the complementarity and focusing on the competition between outlooks is because we have lost a shared acceptance of any overarching context that might encompass them. For Berman, this includes a feel for the ways in which our constitutional system is necessarily entwined with, and subject to, our history. This includes the ways in which our political present and future must be seen as an unfolding of historically defined potentialities carried within our political culture. In that context, the necessary virtues of positivism and natural law can find their rightful place. "Indeed, as a believer in historicity, I would argue that they [positivism and natural law] cannot possibly be reconciled, except in the context of the ongoing history of a given legal order." [16] To think historically requires one to forgo abstract absolutes, at least as stand-alone sources of authority.

---

[14] Berman, "Law and Logos," *DePaul Law Review* Vol. 44, No. 1 (Fall, 1994), p. 154.

[15] Berman, "Toward an Integrative Jurisprudence: Politics, Morality, History," *California Law Review* Vol. 76, No. 4 (July, 1988) p. 783.

[16] Berman, "Law and Logos," 153.

Thinking historically is partly a matter of embracing one's place in a community (or communities) that has a consciousness of itself, with its own ethos and inner life. Historically, this has been the norm, though we surely live with a weakened feel for this sort of belonging and the obligations it confers (some of us having less feel for this than others, of course). But if Berman is right, our constitutional health depends on regaining that consciousness, and along with it, the possibility of reintegrating the different strands of constitutional thought.

Constitutional law must allow for both the active freedom of positivism and the moral guidance of natural law, and it must unfold within the political community's "own historical destiny," as Berman writes, with its own "evolving spirit." That is a tall order in our time of massive social change and extraordinary diversity, both of which present serious challenges to historically rooted, American solidarity. But as Berman ominously adds, "If these qualities are not combined, if they do not interpenetrate each other, the community is threatened with disintegration."[17]

---

[17] Berman, "Law and Logos," 154.

Addendum

AN INTERVIEW
WITH PROFESSOR EPSTEIN

1. You have expressed concern about the danger of fac-
    tionalism at least since the publication of *Takings* in
    1985. But have you been surprised by the depth of
    partisan hostility in the last few years?

    A: I'm not surprised. I'm appalled by it, but that's not
    the same as being surprised. ... Every time I talk
    to my liberal friends—you live on the Upper West
    Side of New York, you can't help but have liberal
    friends—many of them actually don't want to see
    me. They really take it that personally. It's easier to
    get a Catholic to marry a Jew than to get a Repub-
    lican to marry a Democrat. I mean, the polariza-
    tion is really thick and I think it's appalling.

2. You write about the many wrong turns we have taken in terms of our laws and our interpretation of the constitution. At the same time, the nation keeps running. Where do you think our laws, or our constitutional order more broadly, remain soundest?

A: Well, the checks and balances seem to have a lot of influence; the limits of terms—presidents serving for four years, you get turn over in the House and Senate—you get some kind of competitive elections on these things. ... I think at this particular point, there is very serious constitutional stuff, but there is enough gridlock in the Congress that things don't go completely out of whack, though they do go badly out of whack. Where did the constitutional order go wrong? Well, it went wrong, basically, to the extent that they got rid of classical liberal conceptions and made themselves progressives. 1937 was the key year. Before then people had sensible anti-trust law, no particular special labor power of one kind or another, relatively modest subsidies from the government, and by the time you get to 1938, all that is gone.

3. If, as your writings suggest, the constitutional path we have taken has led us into serious trouble, does legislation—which presents the possibility of decisive action based on the will of the people—offer a promising route toward urgently needed reform today?

A: It's always a mixed bag. But you cannot undo constitutional mistakes with legislation even if you try. One of the worst decisions Nino Scalia ever made was [*Employment Division v. Smith*] where he said that neutrality was all that matters in religious regulation and accommodation is not necessary.[1] And it's a disaster, but you try to overturn it by statute and the statute applies here and it doesn't apply there. So it's really hard to say. Legislation can be good or it can be bad and almost never does it get you back to the status quo ante, even if it's well done. And it's always subject to being dissipated by further legislation or negated by rules and regulations issued by departments of revenue and so forth. So without a firm constitutional bedrock in the correct principles, you're always at greater risk than if you have them.

4. In your writings you emphasize that changes in our constitutional order have led to social, as well as economic, damage. If we returned to a state closer to original constitutional values, are you confident that

---

[1] The case concerned religious rights: a fired employee Smith was denied unemployment benefits for having consumed peyote as part of his religious practice. The Supreme Court upheld this denial, rejecting Smith's claim for an exception based on his right to religious freedom. Scalia's decision was based on neutrality in the sense that the drug policy was applied neutrally, regardless of religious affiliation. Epstein criticizes that decision as "dangerously broad" and wrote that it was "wrong to ban any accommodation for any religious beliefs." (See "The War Against Religious Liberty," *The Federalist*, April 9, 2015.)

some of the social damage would be undone— that
our factionalism might relax, for instance, or that
trust in institutions might rebound?

A: Well, it's very difficult to have a clean set of reforms.
So everything goes wrong and you don't know if it's
the reform that's failed or the opposite. All I can say
on any of these things is you can push the needle in
the right direction and it will make a difference. It will
not make everything black or white. To give a simple
illustration, take teenage unemployment. For a long
time we had high minimum wage laws and other
series of preferential treatments which meant that
[managers] were reluctant to hire Black persons over
older persons. ... The way in which to put all this is
every time you make a good reform, it's going to
move the ship, and it's a very big ship, and you have
a long way to turn it, and even if you get one degree
when you need ninety, that one degree is going to
matter. So you have to work for reform on all levels.
There is no margin so small that it doesn't count.

5. Given our deep political divisions, is this a promising
time for a renewed appreciation for the "virtues of
competitive federalism"? (p. 189, *The Classical Liberal Constitution*)

Related: Do you see any likelihood that an ambitious
governor will challenge federal laws in ways that

could lead to the sort of constitutional reform you hope for?

A: I think both of those things are true. Competitive federalism works right now. Look at the population of New York or the population of California; look at the population of Texas; look at the population of Florida. Which way are people moving? Remember, there are huge differences between these states. DeSantis and Abbot have done everything to open up markets. . . . It's competitive federalism that is doing this. And both of these states are vying with the general federal legislation in one form or another. So if you could get the unraveling taking place at the federal level it would no longer be competitive with the basically vast improvements taking place [elsewhere]. In New York, California, and Illinois, all Democratic states, they always lie about the population losses and they always say the other states are missing something. They're not missing anything! I can't tell you the number of my friends who have set up shop in Florida. ... One of the things you should do is look at the Electoral College map from 1940 and compare it to today. New York had 47, now it has 23. I mean it's just a massive population shift all of which are essentially movements from blue to red.

6. Despite the expansion of government's power and reach over the decades, some on both the left and the

right are still frustrated by remaining limitations. Are there any constitutional developments on the horizon that especially worry you?

A: Well, actually the ones on the horizon don't worry me. The two major things that have to do with the public sector is that you have to control administrative discretion. . . . and right now it's very clear that something of that order is going to happen on the Supreme Court. And the second thing is the area of property rights, and the Supreme Court [in] every single case they are taking are pushing back against the synthesis of thirty years ago. ... So what I see on the Supreme Court are incremental signs of improvement. I want to stress: these people are not classical liberals in the sense I am. What they are is skeptical about the administrative state. So they have much less general theory, but the concrete moves they want to make in a cautious and hesitant way are all in the right direction. I can't think of anything they have done that I would regard as dangerous.

7.　Would you be willing to rate our current constitutional health on a scale of 1 to 5, with 1 representing imminent danger and 5 representing perfect health (and explain briefly if possible)?

A: Well, I'm sort of in the middle—about a 3. My view is that the [2024] election is going to be very important, even in terms of long-term political trends. I think that the more extreme branch of the left are intellectually bankrupt. We will never see Diversity, Equity, and Inclusion (DEI) with quite the vehemence that it had the last couple of years. You will never see environmental and social justice stuff taking over corporations the way in which it has. The left has clearly overplayed its hand on many of these kinds of issues. So I would [rate] myself as slightly optimistic, given all the negatives and all the positives.

BOOKS CITED

Richard A. Epstein

Epstein, Richard A. *Takings: Private Property and the Power of Eminent Domain,* Cambridge: Harvard University Press, 1985.

Epstein, Richard A. *The Classical Liberal Constitution: The Uncertain Quest for Limited Government,* Cambridge: Harvard University Press, 2014.

Epstein, Richard A. *Principles for a Free Society: Reconciling Individual Liberty with the Common Good,* New York: Perseus Publishing, 1998.

Epstein, Richard A. *Simple Rules for a Complex Society,* Cambridge: Harvard University Press, 1995.

Epstein, Richard A. *How Progressives Rewrote the Constitution,* Washington, D. C.: Cato Institute, 2006.

Cass R. Sunstein

Sunstein, Cass R. *Legal Reasoning and Political Conflict*, New York/Oxford: Oxford University Press, 1996.

Sunstein, Cass R. *Free Markets and Social Justice*, New York/Oxford: Oxford University Press, 1997.

Sunstein, Cass R. *Simpler: The Future of Government*, New York: Simon and Schuster, 2013.

Sunstein, Cass R. *Worst-Case Scenarios*, Cambridge: Harvard University Press, 2007.

Sunstein, Cass R. *Democracy and the Problem of Free Speech*, New York: The Free Press, 1993.

Sunstein, Cass R. *Liars: Falsehoods and Free Speech in an Age of Deception*, New York/Oxford: Oxford University Press, 2021.

Sunstein, Cass R. *Designing Democracy: What Constitutions Do*, New York/Oxford: Oxford University Press, 2001.

Adrian Vermeule

Sunstein, Cass R. and Adrian Vermeule. *Law and Leviathan: Redeeming the Administrative State*, Cambridge: Harvard University Press, 2020.

Posner, Eric A. and Adrian Vermeule, *The Executive Unbound: After the Madisonian Republic*, New York/Oxford: Oxford University Press, 2010.

Vermeule, Adrian. *Law's Abnegation: From Law's Empire to the Administrative State*, Cambridge: Harvard University Press, 2016.

Vermeule, Adrian. *Common Good Constitutionalism*, Cambridge: Polity Press, 2022.

Other

Berman, Harold J. *Faith and Order: The Reconciliation of Law and Religion.* Emory University Studies in Law and Religion, Grand Rapids: William Eerdmans Publishing Co., 1993.

Bickel, Alexander M. *The Supreme Court and the Idea of Progress,* New London: Yale University Press, 1978.

Dworkin, Ronald. *A Matter of Principle,* Cambridge: Harvard University Press, 1986.

Gray, John. *Liberalism,* Minneapolis: University of Minnesota Press, 1986.

Hobbes, Thomas. *Leviathan* in *Cambridge Texts in the History of Political Thought,* Cambridge University Press, 1991.

Scruton, Roger. *The Meaning of Conservatism,* South Bend: St. Augustine's Press, 2002.

Tierney, Brian. *The Crisis of Church and State 1050–1300,* Toronto: University of Toronto Press, 1988.

ACKNOWLEDGMENTS

Creating a book is a matter of many steps and along the way there are plenty of contributors. Thomas D. Howes, a lecturer in politics at Princeton, read my manuscript and made a number of very useful suggestions and comments. The team at RealClear Publishing provided a great deal of help in making a book out of this, beginning with editors Will Wolfslau and Lauren Magnussen, who guided the project through final edits and production with a sure touch. I was also pleased to work with Sheila Trask, the book's copy editor. Real-Clear's book designer, Josh Taggert, did excellent work in creating the cover for *Vanishing Point*, and similarly fine work on the interior layout. The cover art comes from the artist Jane McKinnon Johnstone, a friend whose work I have long admired.

I also want to thank the three scholars whose work is explored in these pages: Richard A. Epstein, Cass R. Sunstein, and Adrian Vermeule. Their willingness to answer the questions found in the Addendum was genuinely magnanimous, given the heavy demands of their schedules. Finally, I want to thank Helen Byers for her support and companionship throughout the long process of making this book, as well as for her good editorial advice along the way.

ABOUT THE AUTHOR

Edwin C. Hagenstein is a writer and editor with long experiences in publishing. He was the lead editor of *American Georgics: Writings on Farming, Culture, and the Land* (Yale University Press, 2011), and author of *The Language of Liberty: A Citizen's Vocabulary* (Rootstock Publishing, 2020), winner of an Independent Publishers Book Award. He has also published essays, generally on government, in online publications such as *RealClear Public Affairs, The Front Porch Republic,* and *Minding the Campus.* With an interest in woodworking, Hagenstein also wrote *Craft in Common: 30 Years at the Center for Furniture Craftsmanship* (Crow Hill Press, 2023). He lives in northern New Mexico with the artist Helen Byers.